God

LOVES

me

so what!

Guy Rice Doud

God

LOVES

me

so what!

ILLUSTRATED BY

Michael Kilfoy
and R.J. Shay

Publishing House
St. Louis

To our four children:
Seth Thomas, Luke Ryan, Jessica Ruth,
and Zachary Rice.
For when you stop believing in Santa Claus
and ask, "So what?"

He's Everything to Me © 1964 Budjohn Songs Inc. (ASCAP). Adminis-
tered by Copyright Management, Inc. Used by permission.

The Bible text in this publication is from the Good News Bible, the Bible
in TODAY'S ENGLISH VERSION. Copyright © American Bible Society 1966,
1971, 1976. Used by permission.

Copyright © 1992 Concordia Publishing House
3558 S. Jefferson Avenue, St. Louis, MO 63118-3968
Manufactured in the United States of America

Library of Congress Cataloging-in-Publication

Doud, Guy Rice, 1953-
    God loves me—so what! / Guy Rice Doud.
    Summary: Discusses the reality of God and the importance of main-
taining belief in him.
    ISBN 0-570-04572-X
    1. Teenagers—Religious life.   Teenagers—Religious life.
    2. God—Juvenile literature.
BV4531.2.D68   1992
248.8'2—dc20

---

2 3 4 5 6 7 8 9 10   01 00 99 98 97 96 95 94 93 92

Contents

As You Begin . . .

Not long after you stop believing in the Tooth Fairy and Santa Claus, you start having some questions about God. Is He just another character of make-believe? If He really does exist, why is the world the way it is? If He really does exist, does He make a difference when the person you want to go to the dance with doesn't even know you're alive?

This is the time of self-discovery. During these years you come to understand who you are and what that means. You begin to judge yourself, your family, your school, your church. You begin to have lots of questions, and you look lots of different places for answers.

As you grow older, you are faced with an increasing number of choices. Some choices are small, like "Should I eat at McDonald's or Burger King?" Some choices are more important, like "Should I study for that test or go to the movie with a friend?" Some choices are bigger yet, like "What should I do after high school?" and "What career should I choose?"

Then there are choices you may not realize you even have—choices like "What am I going to do about world hunger and poverty?"

But the biggest choice of all is when you stop

and ask yourself this question: "What am I going to do with God?"

I write this book because I believe that God wants to be the major player in your life. The purpose of this book is to help you in the transition between childlike faith and mature faith. It is intended for junior-highers and teenagers, but the principles in this book will work for you regardless of your age.

This isn't a book to be read. It is a book to be lived. Last night, after finishing the last chapter of this book, I went to eat at my favorite Chinese restaurant. The meal was great, as usual. At the end of the meal I got my fortune cookie. My fortune read: "Knowing what to do and not doing it is worse than not knowing it at all." That's what this book is about—having a faith that is active rather than passive.

I have had many of the same doubts and questions you do. I've had many choices to face too. I know that the principles in this book work because I've based my whole life on them. These principles presented in this book aren't original with me, they are taken directly from another book. This other book is also meant to be lived. It's called the *Holy Bible*.

My wife, Tammy, and I have four children. Just the other night our oldest son, Seth, who is nine, lost his last baby tooth. He put the tooth aside to remember to put it under his pillow for the Tooth Fairy. Somehow his tooth got lost. Seth looked everywhere for it, but he couldn't find it. If he couldn't find it, how could the Tooth Fairy give him any money for it?

Tammy had an idea. "Seth," she said, "why don't you leave the Tooth Fairy a note under your pillow. Tell her that your tooth is somewhere in the house. The Tooth Fairy has magic ability to find teeth wherever they are."

Seth thought it was a great idea. He left the Tooth Fairy a note, and sure enough, come morning there was a dollar under his pillow.

Someday Seth will laugh to think that he really believed in the Tooth Fairy, but I hope he'll never think of God as some character of make-believe. Tammy and I hope that as our children grow and make their choices, they will realize how much God loves them and wants to be their very best friend.

That's my wish for you too!

Guy R. Doud

So, Is God Real?

As a kid I was very fat. I mean VERY fat. I was the only kid in fifth grade who had a steel desk. All the rest of the kids had wooden desks. The reason that I had a steel desk was that I had broken two wooden desks. They had literally crumbled beneath my weight! (Of course, my rocking back and forth in them hadn't helped.) So, Mr. Hill, one of the janitors in our school, drove across town to the junior–senior high school and brought back a steel desk just for me. Not only didn't it break, I seemed to fit better in it too . . .

Yeah, I was a big kid. Other kids made fun of me sometimes. It hurt. But there would come a time when I was actually happy to be big . . .

My little brother, Patrick, and I watched him get off the plane. Santa Claus! He had just flown in to the Staples, Minnesota, airport and was going to spend the day walking the city streets, greeting children, and handing out candy canes. Our newspaper, the *Staples World*, said that his visit to town was sponsored by the Staples Chamber of Commerce. Holding my brother's hand I stood among the crowd of kids.

I wondered where Santa's reindeer were and why he didn't come by sleigh. Some other kids must have wondered the same thing because they started yelling, "Where's Rudolph? Where's your sleigh?" I didn't yell, though. I had too much respect for him for that. Patrick let go of my hand and joined the throng that was pressing up against the snow fence to be in the best possible position to greet the man from the North Pole.

Santa, as soon as he was safely on the ground, let off a few "ho, ho, hos," and started handing out candy canes to the boys and girls now crowding around him. I didn't crowd him. After all, I was a kid in fifth grade with a steel desk. I knew that almost none of my classmates believed in Santa anymore. "He's a fake," they said. Some interrogated me: "You don't really believe in Santa Claus anymore, do you, Guy?" When I told them that I did, they just looked at me and asked, "How can you be so dumb?" And this was another one I remember, "Why don't you grow up?"

As I watched Santa greet the children crowding around him, some with their Christmas lists in their hands, I did so this year with a far more skeptical eye. I don't believe anymore, do I? How can I be so dumb? Why don't I grow up?

I stared Santa straight in the eye. I blinked twice. It couldn't be, but it was: Santa was my dad.

My dad! I didn't want to believe it. I wanted to believe in Santa. I wanted him to be real. If I stopped believing, would he stop delivering?

I studied Santa, trying to find reasons why he couldn't be my father. My dad didn't have white eyebrows, did he? Of course, I realized that the beard and the long white hair were probably just wigs, but the eyebrows weren't fake, and they were white. Just as I realized that the eyebrows had probably been colored, I saw Santa give a candy cane to my brother, Pat. It was obvious that Pat didn't have the slightest idea that Santa was Dad. Pat was still a believer. How could he be so dumb?

There was a big part of me that wanted to tell Pat that Santa was our Dad, but I didn't. In fact, I never told anyone that I had stopped believing, just in case that would mean that Santa would quit coming.

Now what does all this have to do with my being fat? Just this: Several years later I took over the position of the town Santa Claus from my father. And I didn't even have to use a pillow—although I did use a little extra Clearasil to cover some of the pimples on my face.

My first year as Santa, my brother was still a believer, but I could only pull the wool over his eyes for one year. The following year I again played Santa. I was sitting in the lobby of the Staples Theatre, greeting the children in the long line waiting to see me. Pat came up to me, sat on my lap, and whispered in my ear, "Hi, Guy" and then he jumped off and ran back into the theater to watch the matinee. My brother no longer believed either.

I guessed that meant that there would be no more gifts from Santa—no more surprises under the tree—no more stockings filled with his little goodies. But I was wrong.

As long as my mother was still alive, and all of our family would come home for Christmas, there was always a little something from Santa under the tree or in our stockings.

Do you still believe in Santa?

You reach an age, don't you, when you no longer believe. There really isn't a Tooth Fairy, or an Easter Bunny. Mickey Mouse and Donald Duck are fakes too.

14

I grew up in Minnesota, where we have lots of lakes. I was told that the heroic woodsman, Paul Bunyan, walked through the land, and wherever his giant boots stepped, he left huge craters in the ground. The rains came and filled up the craters, leaving more than 10,000 lakes. That's how Minnesota came to be "The Land of 10,000 Lakes." Can you believe that I actually believed that?

I did. But I don't any more.

And yet, there is still a part of me that wants to believe in Santa Claus—and Paul Bunyan.

You know, many of us have similar feelings about God. When we're very young, we pray to Him without any doubts. We don't even question. There is a Santa Claus. There is a Tooth Fairy. There is an Easter Bunny. Paul Bunyan is real. I've seen the lakes he made. I've been to Disneyland and Walt Disney World and have seen Mickey Mouse. There is a God and He has a Son and there is a Holy Spirit and they are "three-in-one."

But as we get older—the age differs for different people—we quit making our lists for Santa. We no longer put our old teeth under our pillow. We stop searching for Easter baskets on Easter morning, and we realize that the Paul Bunyan stories are "tall tales," and that Mickey Mouse and Donald Duck are just cartoon characters and are no more real than Charlie Brown and Snoopy.

About this time, way down deep inside, we also begin to wonder if there really is a God and if He has a Son and if there is a Holy Spirit, and how in the world can they be "three-in-one"?

It's okay (even expected of us) to admit that we no longer believe in Santa and the Tooth Fairy, but we don't feel as comfortable admitting that we have some questions and doubts about God (and His Son, and the Spirit—the "three-in-one"). So we often don't admit our doubts and questions. We stuff them down inside and pretend that we don't have them. We're afraid that if we admit our doubts and raise our questions, someone will think that we don't believe, and we've been told that if we don't believe, we won't go to heaven. We have lots of questions about heaven and hell and whether they really exist or not, but just in case they really do, we want to be sure we go to heaven; so we better not admit that we secretly question whether or not they really exist.

Funny, isn't it? The most important questions in the world are "Is God real? and, if He is, What does that mean for me?" and we are often afraid to admit that we ask them. But we do. Everyone has. Everyone must.

We must know why we believe and what we believe. It is not only appropriate to raise questions about God—it is essential.

Well, is there a heaven? Is there a hell? Are

there really angels watching over us? Did God really become a human being named Jesus Christ? Was Jesus really born of a virgin? Did David really kill Goliath? Did Moses part the Red Sea? Did Jesus really turn the water into wine and feed 5,000 people with just 5 loaves and 2 fish? What makes Christians think that their God is the only God? And what about this one: did Jesus really rise from the grave after having been dead for 3 days?

These are only a few of the many questions we begin to ask as we pass from childhood into adulthood. It is so very important that we do not ignore these questions. If God is real, how do I relate with Him as He has revealed Himself to us in the person of Jesus Christ? What kind of relationship do I want to have with Him? If I have faith in Him and desire to have a close relationship with Him, how does that affect my life?

We all reach a point where we must ask ourselves what we believe about God. We can't be neutral. He either exists or He doesn't. There are some people who say, "I am an atheist. I don't believe that there is a God." There are those who say, "Oh, I don't know if there really is a God or not." These people are agnostics. They'll never experience what God has planned for those who believe in Him. Then there are those who say, "I believe in

God. I believe through faith." These people are believers.

Christians believe that God came to earth in the form of a man named Jesus Christ. Christians believe that Jesus was executed, and that through His death, God provided forgiveness of sins for the whole world. There is little doubt that Jesus really lived and was executed. There is historical proof for this. Whether or not He died for our sins and was God, however, must be accepted by faith.

Not long after my 14th birthday (but before I had taken over the role of the town Santa), I remember hearing a pastor paraphrase C. S. Lewis and say, "Either Jesus Christ was who He said He was or He was lying. Or it is possible that He was mentally ill. Or . . . it is possible that He was who He said He was. Which is it?" I have never forgotten that. And then the pastor asked, "What do you believe about Jesus?"

A song that had become popular at that time was "He's Everything to Me." As I wondered what to believe about Jesus, I remember hearing these words from the chorus of the song:

'Til by faith I met Him face to face
And I felt the wonder of His grace,
Then I knew that He was more than just
A God who didn't care, who lived a way up
there.
Now He walks beside me day by day,

18

Ever watching o'er me lest I stray,
Helping me to find that narrow way.
He's everything to me!

Who was Jesus to me? Was He just someone "way up there" who "really didn't care?" Jesus made some pretty bold claims about who He is. Jesus claimed to be the fulfillment of the Old Testament prophecies concerning the Messiah. He claimed to be the Christ. He claimed to be the Savior. He claimed to be the way and the truth and the life, and said that no one could get to the Father except through Him. In fact, Jesus claimed to be God.

I had to either believe Jesus' claim, with the help of the Holy Spirit, or reject it. By choosing not to make up my mind about it, I would be choosing to make up my mind against Jesus. If I believed the claims of Jesus, what would that mean for my life? How would believing in Jesus make a difference at school? at home? with my friends in the neighborhood? How would believing in Jesus affect me when I was alone with my thoughts, unable to sleep at night?

No one could decide for me what I would believe about Jesus. No matter how much my mother and my sister, who were committed Christians, wanted me to believe in Jesus, they couldn't believe for me. Although I had gone through confirmation class at church, I still had not really made up my mind as to what I would do with Jesus. Jesus was just someone I knew about in my head, but I hadn't realized how much the things I'd been learning really meant in my life.

I remember so well when I was about your age, realizing that Jesus was Lord of my whole life. I knew that being a follower of Jesus brought with it a responsibility to live for Him. I knew, too, that He had promised to walk with me. It was up to me to walk with Him.

Do you really believe in Jesus? So what? What difference does that make in your life? How do you develop a faith that works? We don't just need more head knowledge about God, we need to know how to make God the major player in our lives.

Do you have a hard time believing that God made the world and is in control of everything, including your life? Think about it a minute. Is it not actually harder to believe that the world all happened by chance?

I wear a watch on my wrist. (It's a Mickey Mouse watch from Disneyland.) Although I've never taken it apart, I believe that inside the watch are many little pieces. Each one functions just perfectly to help my watch keep the accurate time it does. What would happen if I took my watch apart and threw it in a paper bag? Imagine all the pieces of my watch—including the Mickey

Mouse hands—lying in the bottom of the bag. Let's say that I then began to shake the bag. How long do you think I would have to shake before all the pieces of my watch fell correctly back into place?

There are some people who believe that is how the universe was formed. It just happened by chance. Everything just fell into place. I find that impossible to believe. If all the pieces of my watch could never fall into place, what's the possibility of the world, with all of its intricacy, ever just happening by chance, with everything just falling into place? If my watch could ever be reassembled, it would take a watchmaker to do it. And it took God to make the world. God made you, and He made me. You are far more complex (and so am I) than any watch—even a Rolex! You didn't happen by chance, You are one of a kind.

God showed us what He was like when He came to earth as Christ. What He showed us was that He is love. There is nothing He wants to do more than love us. The first step in responding to God's love is believing in Him.

Do you believe in Jesus Christ? If you have doubts, admit them. That's okay. Your faith is never going to grow unless you face your doubts and confront them. Everyone has had doubts. A guy by the name of Frederick Buechner wrote, "Doubt is the ants in the pants of faith; it keeps it alive and moving." How about that? Ants in the pants of faith? As a school teacher, I've seen lots of kids who have seemed to have ants in their pants, but "ants in the pants of faith?" That sure is an interesting way of putting it!

I remember a girl in my Sunday school class who wondered if Jesus really cared about her. A friend of mine asked me once, "Guy, do you really think that God answers prayer?" He had doubts. I knew a young guy who said he found it really hard to believe some of the stories in the Bible—like the one about Jonah and the big fish. Are there any stories that you have questions about?

John the Baptist had doubts. He wondered whether or not Jesus was the Son of God (Luke 7:18–23). Asaph, who wrote Psalm 73, had some doubt. He wrote: "Is it for nothing, then, that I have kept myself pure and have not committed sin? / O God, You have made me suffer all day long; every morning You have punished me."

Have you ever felt like Asaph? "Why should I be a Christian? What good does it do?" Realize that such doubts are normal. Realize, too, that God doesn't love you less when you have doubts. God understands, and He accepts you—doubts and all. Confront your doubts. Share them with someone you know who has a strong faith in God. Maybe they'll tell you how they handled their

22

doubts. They may have had, or have, some of the same ones as you.

You might have some questions and doubts that no one will ever be able to answer well enough to satisfy you. But keep searching for answers. There are some questions you will probably have to ask God Himself. The Bible tells us that some-day we will see Him face to face. Then all our questions will be answered! In the meantime, tell God your doubts and ask Him to keep your faith strong. He will!

The journey of faith begins when God the Holy Spirit works faith in you and you believe in Jesus as your Savior. Allow that faith to affect the way you live. Live like you believe. Act like you believe. Believe like you believe. As you do, your faith will grow. The more faith you use, the more you receive. It's one of the really interesting things about God. It's like His love—the more you give away, the more you get back.

That's what the rest of this book is about: How should the faith I have in Jesus Christ affect my life? How can faith help me in the choices I have to make? How does faith help me accept my uniqueness? How does faith influence what goes on in my family? How does my faith in Jesus in-fluence my relationships at school and with my friends? Good questions! "God" questions!

Our children are all still young enough that

they believe in Santa. Our oldest child, however, is beginning to question the truth about old St. Nick. No doubt he will soon no longer believe in the man from the North Pole. Yet Tammy and I hope and pray that as each of our children quit believing in Santa Claus (and the Tooth Fairy and all the other characters of fantasy), that instead of including God in this list of make-believe, they will have a solid relationship with Him and build their lives on the firm foundation of faith in Jesus Christ.

He is, after all, a "rock that doesn't roll."

That's my prayer for you too!

So, What Are the A B C's?

I had the cruise set at 55 (really!), and I was driving home with three of the kids in the car—two in the back seat and one in front with me. Seth, our oldest, was feeling rather proud to be sitting up front with Dad. He and Luke had argued about whose turn it was to sit up in front, and Seth had won. Jessica, safely buckled into her car seat in the back, was still too young to demand much more than food, a clean diaper, and sleep.

I reached over to adjust the radio, when suddenly the passenger door opened and Seth was seemingly being sucked out of the car. It all happened so fast. My right hand immediately left the radio and reached for Seth, who seemed to be halfway out the door.

Luke screamed, "Seth-h-h-h . . . !" And Jessica—knowing something terrible was happening—began to cry.

I pulled Seth back into the car, slammed the door and locked it, and immediately demanded that Seth put on his seat belt. I yelled at Luke and told him to make sure his seat belt was on. I knew that Jessica was safe, but in the process of scolding Seth rather severely, I put my seat belt on too.

"How many times have I told you not to play with the door?" I yelled at Seth. My heart was beating wildly. I don't think I expected him to say, "Oh, a hundred or so times," but I did want an answer. When he didn't give me an answer, I asked it again: "Well, how many times have I told you not to play with the door?"

"I don't know," he mumbled.

"You could have died! Your body would have been strewn all over the highway! Is that what you want?"

"No," Seth said, and he began to join Jessica with his tears. My heart melted. He must have been frightened too.

"Honey, I love you, and I don't want to see you hurt."

Seth confessed: "I was just opening the door

to get some light, so I could find the piece of candy I dropped on the floor."

So that was it. A piece of candy. "Honey, we'll find the candy when we get home, but never, never, never, *never,* open the door of a moving car again. You could die."

"Okay, Dad, I promise, I'll never do it again." Seth seemed sincere. My heart was beginning to slow down a beat or two.

"Dad, Seth was really being stupid, wasn't he?" This was Luke's offering from the back seat.

"That's okay, Luke, he doesn't need you to tell him." And as I said that, I realized how much I sounded like my parents.

When Seth started out the door of the car, I didn't have to stop and think about what I should do. I didn't have to say, "Well, now, I wonder if I should reach over there and pull him back into the car? Would that be a wise thing to do? What do you think, Luke, and Jessica, what do you think? Should I stop and call home and ask Mom what she thinks? Should I attempt to save him, or shouldn't I?" It was very obvious: I had to save him. My reaction was immediate and did not require any thought or deliberation. It was almost a reflex action—like when you quickly withdraw your hand when you feel something burning hot— or when you steady yourself when you begin to slip on ice.

Most things in life, however, are not that easy. Usually we have choices. Lots of them. Very few reactions need to be as quick as my action rescuing Seth. Most of the time we can stop and wonder. We can even call home.

The strange thing, though, is that often we aren't aware of all the choices we have. We simply do things without really thinking about them. Instead of opening the door to have some light in the car to find his lost candy, Seth could have asked me to turn the dome light on. Obviously Seth hadn't stopped to really think about what he was doing.

When I was a kid, my family used to tease me that I had "my head in the clouds" half the time. In other words, I often did things without thinking about them first. I remember the cold winter (below zero!) Saturday afternoon I stood in front of the Staples Theatre waiting for the doors to open so I could get in and see the matinee. As I stood there freezing, I noticed the black wrought iron rail that went around the stairs leading to a basement office. All of a sudden the rail called out to me: "Come here, little boy, and put your tongue on me! It feels so good!"

I walked over to the rail and put my tongue on it. The theater manager opened the doors at the same moment I realized that my tongue was frozen to the rail, and that it was going hurt like crazy to rip it off. I must have been a sorry sight: bent over, tongue fully extended from my mouth, and frozen to the rail. I looked at the theater manager out of the corner of my right eye. My eye begged for help, but he didn't appear to see me. Some of the other kids arriving for the matinee just laughed when they saw me frozen there.

I was right. It did hurt like crazy when I ripped my tongue from the rail. I was sure my tongue would never be the same again. It hurt so bad I knew that I wasn't going to be able to eat any popcorn. As I paid for my ticket to the matinee, the theatre manager said, "I bet you're about the 10th kid who has put his tongue on that rail this winter. Hurts, doesn't it?"

Well, if he knew that so many kids had had their tongues frozen to the rail, why in the world hadn't he put up a sign warning us about it? "Caution: Sticking your tongue on this rail can be hazardous to your tongue and may prevent you from eating popcorn." Or something like that.

But I had a choice, didn't I? No one forced me to put my tongue on the rail, but once I had done it my choices were severely limited. I sure wish I had thought a little more before I had done it. I certainly have never done it again . . .

That's the way life is: we have lots of choices. Unfortunately, many times we do things without really thinking first—without really planning the

best strategy. Seth didn't really think before he opened the door, and I didn't really think before becoming one with the iron rail. This is why it would be a good idea to review our A B C's . . .

The following model is used to explain circumstances and how we handle them:

 Something happens.

 We decide how we are going to react to what has happened.

 We react.

Pretty basic, huh? But think back to the story about Seth opening the car door. What happened?

 Seth lost his candy. Since it was dark in the car, and he couldn't see the floor,

 Seth decided to open the door so that the dome light would aid him in his search.

 Seth opened the door and almost got strewn all over the highway. (And he would have if Dad had not rescued him!)

Seth obviously didn't spend much time on B, and because of it, could easily have died. Many times our reactions (C) are like Seth's—they occur without much real thought. Instead of "ready, aim, fire!" often it is "ready, fire, aim!" This can be even more hazardous to your health than putting your tongue on an iron rail.

At least Seth had an explanation for why he opened the door. How about my example of my tongue on the wrought-iron rail?

 Guy is waiting outside the movie theater. He is cold, and he is bored. Guy sees a wrought-iron rail. It appears to be calling out to him.

 Guy immediately goes over and places his tongue on the rail.

It is quite apparent that I skipped B all together. Skipping B can get us into some pretty serious trouble.

How does this relate to our relationship with Jesus? Let's look at our model again:

 Something happens. A circumstance occurs.

 God's Spirit guides me in deciding how I should respond.

 I think or act as God's Spirit has guided.

Of course, there are times when plain old

common sense works best. I doubt that God's Spirit would have given me much help in deciding whether or not to stick my tongue on the rail, but when it comes to knowing how to live like a follower of Christ in school and at home, the Spirit is just waiting to be our guide.

Jesus told us about the Spirit. Jesus said, "When, however, the Spirit comes, who reveals the truth about God, He will lead you into all the truth. He will not speak on His own authority, but He will speak of what He hears and will tell you of things to come" (John 16:13). The Holy Spirit wants to be our guide in all the important decisions in our lives (and in ones that don't even seem all that important).

Look what Paul says about the Holy Spirit: "What I say is this: let the Spirit direct your lives, and you will not satisfy the desires of the human nature. For what our human nature wants is opposed to what the Spirit wants, and what the Spirit wants is opposed to what our human nature wants. These two are enemies, and this means that you cannot do what you want to do. If the Spirit leads you, then you are not subject to the Law" (Galatians 5:16–18).

What Paul is talking about here is "B" in our model. Notice how he says that "what our human nature wants is opposed to what the Spirit wants." This is the sin nature with which we were born. In the last chapter we talked about doubt. When I was a young adult I wondered why God allowed evil in the world. Why didn't God stop Adam and Eve from sinning? If He had, He wouldn't have had to send His Son to die, so why didn't He? These were some of my questions.

Paul answers these questions in the same chapter from Galatians mentioned above: "As for you, my brothers, you were called to be free. But do not let this freedom become an excuse for letting your physical desires control you. Instead, let love make you serve one another. . . . if you act like wild animals, hurting and harming each other, then watch out, or you will completely destroy one another" (Galatians 5:13–15).

God loved us so much He gave us freedom. He lets us figure out how we are going to respond to His love. He lets us decide our own B in the model. Sure, He could have made us in such a way that we would have no choice of whether or not to do anything wrong, but if He had made us that way, we wouldn't be human. If He had made us that way we would be like robots, and we would never be able to experience love. Love cannot be forced from someone, it must come willingly.

There was this girl I thought I was in love with in high school. I would see her, and immediately I could feel my heart beating through my shirt. I wanted her to love me back, or at least acknowledge my presence . . . I could just picture her sitting beside me in my car. I could just see my arm around her shoulder. I could just imagine her holding my hand. Trouble was, she was doing all these things with some other guy (no pun intended). Could I have kidnaped her and forced her to be my girlfriend? Certainly not. Love cannot be forced.

When I was in junior high school I read a book called *Jonathan Livingston Seagull* by Richard Bach. I remember the theme of the book being this: "If you love something, set it free; if it comes back to you, it is yours; if it doesn't, it was never yours to begin with." The book became a best-seller, and bumper stickers soon began appearing with that quote. My friends and I, however, got a kick out of the bumper sticker that read: "If you love something, set it free; if it comes back to you, it's yours; if it doesn't, hunt it down and shoot it!"

Of course, the quote related to young sea gulls leaving home, but the sea gulls were merely symbols for people. If you love someone you must give that person freedom to make choices. Parents learn that they have to allow their children freedom to form their own values and beliefs. No matter how much Mom and Dad may want their children to believe what they believe, the children

35

have to make up their own minds and make their own decisions.

God, our heavenly Father, loved us so much that He gave us freedom. He knew that we could never love Him unless we were free to do so. Unfortunately, Adam and Eve made some wrong choices, and people have been making bad choices ever since. Despite the bad choices, the sin, God has never stopped loving us. He didn't hunt us down and shoot us! He sent Christ to redeem us, and has provided the Holy Spirit to help guide us in all the decisions we have to make.

What happens if we don't pay any attention to the Spirit and make the wrong decisions? Paul mentions these things too: "What human nature does is quite plain. It shows itself in immoral, filthy, and indecent actions; in worship of idols and witchcraft. People become enemies and they fight; they become jealous, angry, and ambitious. They separate into parties and groups; they are envious, get drunk, have orgies, and do other things like these. I warn you now as I have before: those who do these thing will not possess the kingdom of God." (Galatians 5:19–21).

Wow! I've experienced many of the things listed above. How about you? You see, these things result from not allowing God's Spirit to control the B part of our lives. If our faith is really going to make a difference in our lives, we need to work on B—allowing God's Spirit to guide us and control us.

Look what happens when we do allow the Spirit to guide us: "But the Spirit produces love, joy, peace, patience, kindness, goodness, faithfulness, humility, and self-control. There is no law against such things as these" (Galatians 5:22–23).

Wow! These are things that I want in my life! These are the fruits of godly living—of allowing the Holy Spirit to control the B part of our lives.

Growing up, one of the things that was hard for me to understand as I asked questions about my faith was the work of the Holy Spirit. I never felt that the Spirit was given much attention. We talked a lot in church and Sunday school about God and Jesus, but the only time I heard much about the Spirit was when we recited the Apostles' Creed. Then one Christmas my sister gave me a good study Bible, and I happened to read about the Holy Spirit coming to the believers at Pentecost. My Bible said something about the Holy Spirit being the "often forgotten member of the Trinity" and then made the comment that "the Holy Spirit is as important as God the Father and God the Son." Really? I talked to a pastor friend of mine and he said, "Guy, the Holy Spirit is the Christian's power source! He is what makes our light shine!"

I started thinking a lot about God's Spirit being the power source. I wondered if God's power was really available to me.

At this time, I was manager of our high school basketball team. I loved the home games because it was great having the crowd on our side. The coach said that a good spirited hometown crowd could add 10–15 points to a team's score. During the game, I could literally feel the spirit of the crowd as they cheered on the home team. The spirit in the gymnasium bound the local fans and players together. It was awesome. There was power in the spirit of the crowd.

Years later, I would realize that God's Spirit wants to control our lives in such a way that we always have the home-field advantage in the everyday and extraordinary circumstances of our lives. God's Spirit is what joins us with Him, and with other members of the Christian community. The Spirit is awesome and powerful!

When we allow the Spirit to control our lives and have the home-field advantage, we begin to grow in our relationship with Christ. It has a dramatic effect on the way we live. Going back to our A B C model, our B decides our C. When we yield to God's will for us in individual situations, we are yielding to God. We are giving God the home-field advantage in our lives rather than giving it to the devil.

The following story illustrates the home-field advantage.

Adam, Brent, and Josh are playing darts in the basement of Adam's house and listening to music. Adam's parents are gone and won't be back until after midnight. Adam has convinced his parents that he is old enough to be at home by himself and that his two friends can spend the night at his house without getting into trouble. Adam throws a dart. It ricochets off the dart board and lands a few feet to the right, at the base of Adam's father's liquor cabinet. Suddenly, Adam has an idea. "Do you guys want to have some cocktails?" he asks with a grin.

"Won't we get in trouble?" Brent asks.

"No, we'll drink vodka, it doesn't make your breath stink," Adam answers. "No one will ever know. Besides, we'll be asleep long before they get home."

"But won't your dad notice that some of it is missing?" Brent questions.

"Heck no, he has so much booze that he won't even notice that some is gone. Come on! Let's have some drinks!"

"Sounds great!" Brent joins in.

Josh stands frozen. He doesn't want to drink. He knows that Adam's parents trust them. He knows that his parents trust him. He has signed a form in school pledging that, as a mem-

ber of a school athletic team, he will not use drugs or alcohol. He knows that disobedience is a sin. He knows, too, that if he doesn't have a drink with his friends they will probably ridicule him and he'll feel left out.

"Do you want yours with 7-Up or with orange juice?" Adam asks.

"Orange juice, ple-e-ease . . . ," answers Brent, trying hard to be a comedian and speaking loudly to be heard over the music.

"What about you, Josh, what do you want with your vodka?"

But before Josh can answer, the phone rings.

"Turn down the music! It's probably my parents," Adam shouts as he runs to answer the phone. "Hello," Adam answers. He listens. "Oh, hi, Mom." He makes faces at Josh and Brent as he listens to his mother. "Yes, Mom, we're being good. No wild parties, Mom! No dancing women! We're being angels!" He listens some more. "Okay, Mom . . . yeah . . . we'll be in bed before you get home. See you in the morning. Bye." He hangs up the phone and returns to his friends.

"Well-l-l . . . Joshy . . . did you ever tell me what you wanted with your vodka?" Adam asks.

Josh doesn't answer immediately. There is

a big knot in the pit of his stomach. What should he do?

Let's examine what has happened. Josh had been having a good time playing darts, but suddenly he wasn't having a good time anymore. It's like riding your bike on a beautiful day with the sun shining brightly. The skies are blue and there are no clouds in the sky. Suddenly, you hear a mammoth "kaboom!" and soon you are pedaling through a half a foot of water and you are soaked clean through. What happened? The weather changed. A storm front moved in, forcing the beautiful weather away. The same thing had happened for Josh. His good time was suddenly not so good anymore, and his spirit was no longer happy.

There is good weather and bad weather, and sometimes we confront both within a matter of minutes. The weather is like the Spirit. There is a good Spirit and a bad spirit. There is God's way, and there is the devil's way. The Bible tells us: "Be alert, be on watch! Your enemy, the Devil, roams around like a roaring lion, looking for someone to devour. Be firm in your faith and resist him, because you know that your fellow believers in all the world are going through the same kind of sufferings" (1 Peter 5:8–9).

When we think of Satan—or the devil, as many people call him—we often picture a guy in

41

a red suit, with horns and a tail, holding a pitch-fork in his hand. The truth is that Satan attacks us in the ways we expect the least. The Bible says Satan may even disguise himself as a good angel. He might even be disguised as a pastor or priest. When Peter told Jesus that He shouldn't say that He was going to die, Jesus said, "Satan, get behind me!" There are times when Satan tries to get at us through our best friends. He loves to send bad weather into our lives, and he is always looking for an opportunity to fill our lives with his bad spirit. When we allow him to do that we no longer have the home-field advantage.

Now, back to the story about Josh. Look at what Adam did:

 "Ah, there's my father's liquor cabinet."

 "Wouldn't it be fun to drink?"

 "I'm going to have some drinks!"

Brent reacted in this fashion:

 "I have an offer to drink."

 "Can I do it without getting into trouble? Adam assures me that I can."

 "All right! Let's party!"

"Well, Josh," Adam asks, "what do you want with your vodka?" Josh thinks:

 "I have an offer to drink."

 "My promises to my parents, Adam's parents, my coach—they mean a lot to me. For me to break those promises would be wrong. I have to risk Adam and Brent being angry with me. Being at peace with myself and with God is more important to me than pleasing my friends."

 "I don't care to drink, you guys. And if you're going to drink, it's probably best that I go home."

Adam and Brent are shocked. Josh is usually a good sport about almost everything. The weather has changed again. Now there is a cold front moving in. Josh, however, feels better. He has withstood a giant gust of wind, and he is still standing. Adam and Brent, however, feel somewhat betrayed by their friend. They don't want him to leave, but they don't want him to get down on them for drinking either. They've made up their minds that they are going to drink, and they don't want anyone to stop them.

You see, what Josh has done has given God's Spirit the home-field advantage, and as a result of it, he feels the added power that comes with the Spirit's guidance.

It is important to note the following: Even if

you give God's Spirit the home-field advantage, the result might still seem crummy. In this case, Josh's friends are angry at him, and what was supposed to be a fun evening isn't fun anymore. It's like winning the game but losing your star player. When you feel this way, it is important to remember the long-term results and rewards of decisions rather than their immediate, seemingly negative consequences. No doubt, if Josh's friendship with Adam and Brent is strong it will survive this episode. If it doesn't, then in the long run it probably isn't the kind of friendship worth having.

What would have happened if Josh had reacted this way:

 "I have an offer to drink."

 "I know I've promised that I won't, but no one will ever know that I have. I don't want Adam and Brent to be upset with me. Besides, I know a lot of other guys on the team who drink, and don't all kids disobey their parents as part of growing up?"

 "Make me a screwdriver-r-r-r, Adam!"

Well, if Josh had reacted that way, he would have blown it! He would have taken away the Spirit's home-field advantage. He would have given the advantage to the visiting team—just like

44

Adam and Brent had done. What happens if you do the wrong C?

Jesus taught about the Spirit. He said, "And when He comes, He will prove to the people of the world that they are wrong about sin and about what is right and about God's judgment. . . . When, however, the Spirit comes, who reveals the truth about God, . . . He will not speak on His own authority, but He will speak of what He hears and will tell you of things to come. He will give Me glory, because He will take what I say and tell it to you. All that My Father has is Mine; that is why I said that the Spirit will take what I give Him and tell it to you" (John 16:8, 13–15).

Jesus said that the same Spirit who is available to guide us and provide us with the truth can also convince us of God's goodness. In other words, there is forgiveness when we blow it. God still loves us. He still wants us on His team. He still longs to give us the home-field advantage.

God has a storehouse of power available for us through His Spirit. His Spirit will help us control the weather and provide us with the home-field advantage.

If you are cruising down the road at 65 miles an hour—I mean, 55 miles an hour—you don't have to think twice about whether or not to grab your son who is flying out the door. But most things in life aren't that easy. Most things involve choices: A, B, C. God wants to be involved in those choices. He wants you to give His Spirit the home-field advantage.

So, Let's Play!

The trip home from Adam's had been ugly for Josh. All the way home he could still hear Adam and Brent's words ringing in his ears. They had called him some really rotten names when he refused to drink with them. He stayed around for a while, but then Adam said that his dad had an X-rated video, and he put it in the VCR. That's when Josh decided to leave. Adam and Brent questioned his masculinity. "Grow up, Josh!" they said. "Be a man!" Josh had finally left Adam's house without even saying good-bye, and on the long walk home he had wiped more than a couple tears from his eyes.

Josh walked into the kitchen of his home. "Hi, Mom," he said.

"Well, hello, honey, what are you doing home? I thought you were going to be spending the night at Adam's?"

"Yeah, well, it didn't work out," Josh said.

"What happened?" Mom asked.

"I don't really feel like talking about it, okay?"

"Well, Josh, I'd like to know what happened. Please tell me."

"Please, Mom. Just back off and give me some space."

"I wish you felt like you could trust me to talk about it, Josh."

"It's not that I don't trust you, Mom, I just need to think about some things, okay?"

"Well, maybe later we can talk."

"Maybe later," Josh said, "but now I think I'm just going to go to bed. Good night, Mom." Josh walked over and gave his mother a kiss.

His mom gave him a hug and said, "I love you, honey."

"I love you, too, Mom."

Josh ran up the stairs to his bedroom and shut the door. He threw his backpack on a chair, took off his coat, turned on some tunes, and lay down on the bed. He lay there staring at the ceiling. Lots of thoughts were running through his head: I made the right decision; or did I? I should have stayed with Adam and Brent;

things will never again be the same with my friends. No one will ever know the sacrifice I've made. Is doing the right thing worth it?

His body seemingly operating by remote control, Josh suddenly rose from the bed, walked over to his dresser and started emptying the change from his jean pockets. One of the coins rolled a few inches and finally rolled into a book sitting at the end of the dresser. Josh looked at the book. His grandparents had given it to him for his birthday—a new study Bible. He picked up the Bible. He hadn't really looked at it all that much. In fact, he had been rather disappointed with the gift. He would rather have had a new compact disc or even a sweatshirt or something. It was like his grandparents, though. They were always talking about Jesus as though they were close personal friends or something. Even Josh's parents thought that his grandparents got a little carried away at times.

Josh picked up the Bible. He opened it. His Grandfather had written in the inside front cover: "To our grandson, Joshua Ryan Anderson, you are the apple of God's eye. He loves you so! He is watching over you. Remember, Josh, 'This book will keep you from sin, or sin will keep you from this book.' Happy Birthday! Love, Gram and Grampa Anderson (Matthew 5:1–16)."

Whenever Josh went to stay with his grand-

49

parents, they would have a short devotion time before going to bed. Grandpa would read something from the Bible and share a few thoughts about it. Then they would always say some prayers, praying especially for Josh. Once his grandfather had asked him, "Josh, would you like to pray?" Josh had answered, "No, I think you've covered it all." Josh didn't really feel comfortable praying in front of others. About the only prayers he ever really said were table grace and the Lord's Prayer before going to sleep, but his grandparents talked to God and Jesus as though He were sitting right there with them.

Josh stared at his grandfather's note for a few moments. He read it again: "Joshua Ryan Anderson, you are the apple of God's eye. He loves you so! He is watching over you. Remember, Josh, 'This book will keep you from sin, or sin will keep you from this book.' " Josh thought about that for a moment, and then noticed that his grandfather had listed a Scripture reference: Matthew 5:1–16. He took the Bible over to his bed, propped up his pillows and opened the Bible to that passage. He read:

> Jesus saw the crowds and went up a hill, where He sat down. His disciples gathered around Him, and He began to teach them:
>
> "Happy are those who know they are spir-

itually poor; the kingdom of heaven belongs to them! . . .

"Happy are those who are humble; they will receive what God has promised!

"Happy are those whose greatest desire is to do what God requires; God will satisfy them fully!

"Happy are those who are merciful to others; God will be merciful to them!

"Happy are the pure in heart; they will see God!

"Happy are those who work for peace; God will call them His children!

"Happy are those who are persecuted because they do what God requires; the kingdom of heaven belongs to them!

"Happy are you when people insult you and persecute you and tell all kinds of evil lies against you because you are My followers. Be happy and glad, for a great reward is kept for you in heaven. This is how the prophets who lived before you were persecuted.

"You are like salt for all mankind. But if salt loses its saltiness, there is no way to make it salty again. It has become worthless, so it is thrown out and people trample on it.

"You are like light for the whole world. A city built on a hill cannot be hid. No one lights a lamp and puts it under a bowl; instead he puts it on the lampstand, where it gives light for everyone in the house. In the same way your light must shine before people, so that they will see the good things you do and praise your Father in heaven."

The verse that read, "In the same way your light must shine before people, so that they will see the good things you do and praise your Father in heaven," was underlined. Gramps, Josh smiled. Josh had heard this entire passage in church many times, but the words had never sunk in before. He looked over the passage. This verse caught his eye: "Happy are you when people insult you and persecute you and tell all kinds of evil lies against you because you are My followers. Be happy and glad, for a great reward is kept for you in heaven."

Josh had never really thought of himself as a follower of Christ before. He believed in Jesus, but didn't get really carried away with it or anything. Most Sundays he would rather sleep in instead of getting up to go to church.

Josh looked at the verse his grandfather had underlined, "Your light must shine." Without even realizing what he was doing, Josh closed his eyes and said, "Jesus, I need Your help right now. Please help me. I want my light to shine for You, but You have to help me."

No bombs exploded or anything like that,

but Josh suddenly felt much more at peace. He had made the right decision. It hurt. It may damage his friendship with Adam and Brent forever, but for some strange reason he started to feel better.

What has happened? Remember our A B C model from the last chapter?

 Josh is faced with the temptation to drink alcohol and watch a pornographic movie.

 Josh decides to go home.

 Josh is ridiculed by his friends, comes home, tries to avoid his mother, and retires to his room.

At this point Josh is not a happy camper. Even though he made the right decision (B), he made the decision on his own strength and power. As a result, Josh feels like he is in a blizzard. What has to occur to drive out the storm front? When Josh reads the Bible and prays, peace begins to return to his life. Oh, sure, he still feels upset and hurt, but God's Spirit begins to soothe his hurts and calm his spirit. When Josh reads the Bible and prays, he has once again given the Spirit the home-field advantage.

Most situations aren't as dramatic as the one Josh faced, but nonetheless, the same A B C principle applies. B is really the heart of the matter. This is where our choices make the big difference. Two forces are always fighting to control our lives—the Spirit and the devil. What we must do is give God's Spirit the advantage. How do we do this? Let's illustrate it with another acronym: PLAY.

We all love to play! But how can our "play" give God center court in our lives? Check this out:

P Pray

L Learn

A Act

Y Yield

If we are really going to have a faith that works—one that makes a difference on Friday and Saturday nights—we must "play" God's way. This is where spiritual growth enters the picture. When God's Spirit helps us live for Him, our lives change. We start to do things God's way, rather than our way or the world's way. This change that God's Spirit works in us is known as *sanctification.* God wants to "set us apart" from the rest of the world so that we become righteous.

But the choice is ours. The choice is yours: A B C. What are you going to do with B? Look what the Bible says about your choices: "Surely you know that when you surrender yourselves as slaves to obey someone, you are in fact the slaves of the master you obey—either of sin, which results in death, or of obedience, which results in being put right with God. But thanks be to God! For though at one time you were slaves to sin, you have obeyed with all your heart the truths found in the teaching you received. You were set free from sin and became the slaves of righteousness" (Romans 6:16–18).

You see, Christians are those who have chosen to follow Christ, to make Him their master. When we follow Jesus, He expects changes in our lives. Look:

> What shall we say, then? Should we continue to live in sin so that God's grace will increase? Certainly not! We have died to sin—how then can we go on living in it? For surely you know that when we were baptized into union with Christ Jesus, we were baptized into union with His death. By our baptism, then, we were buried with Him and shared His death, in order that, just as Christ was raised from death by the glorious power of the Father, so also we might live a new life.
>
> For since we have become one with Him in dying as He did, in the same way we shall be one with Him by being raised to life as He

was. And we know that our old being has been put to death with Christ on His cross, in order that the power of the sinful self might be destroyed, so that we should no longer be the slaves of sin. (Romans 6:1–6)

Wow! We share Christ's new life! Paul, who wrote the letter to the Romans, gets right to the point in verse 12 of the same chapter: "Sin must no longer rule in your mortal bodies, so that you obey the desires of your natural self. Nor must you surrender any part of yourselves to sin to be used for wicked purposes. Instead, give yourselves to God, as those who have been brought from death to life, and surrender your whole being to Him to be used for righteous purposes. Sin must not be your master; for you do not live under law but under God's grace" (Romans 6:12–14).

For us to get to the point where sin no longer rules in our mortal bodies, the following steps can be helpful:

P Pray

L Learn

A Act

Y Yield

Pray

Remember how Josh felt better after he said a simple prayer to God? Prayer is our direct line to the Maker of the universe. No one loves you more or understands you better than God does, and He is available to talk with you at any time and at any place.

A few days later Josh was playing basketball after school. There were only a few seconds left in the game, and Josh's team was behind by two points. The forward threw Josh the ball, and he quickly started down the court, but was fouled in the process. It was a two-shot foul. Josh needed to make both shots to tie the game. He stood at the line and gazed at the basket. He shot. It was good! Now he needed to make this next basket to tie the game and send it into overtime. The ref handed Josh the ball. Josh prayed silently, Please, God! Help me make this basket. *Josh shot. The ball hit the rim and bounced into the outstretched arms of an opposing player. The buzzer rang. The game was over, and Josh's team had lost by one point.*

Had God failed to hear Josh's prayer? If God had heard it, how come He didn't answer it?

What about your prayer life? Is it powerful and awesome, or rather weak and forgotten? Do you spend much time in prayer? Do you believe that God really hears and answers prayers? If we are going to allow the Spirit to control the B part of our lives, we must develop an active prayer life.

The Bible says, "Be joyful always, pray at all times, be thankful in all circumstances. This is what God wants from you in your life in union with Christ Jesus" (1 Thessalonians 5:16–18).

The next time Josh saw Grandpa Anderson, he asked him, "Grandpa, how come God doesn't answer some prayers?"

Grandpa looked at Josh and smiled warmly. "I heard it explained once that God answers prayers in one of three ways. He says 'Go,' 'No,' or 'Grow.' When He says 'Go,' He has said yes. Just like there are times when your parents say no because they know what's best for you, God sometimes says no too. And there are times when God says, 'Grow.' That's like when your Dad tells you you can buy that new stereo after you've saved up enough money for it. There are times, you see, when God tells you to wait until a better time too."

Josh sat for a few moments, letting his grandfather's words sink in. "You know, Josh," his grandpa continued, "one of the things it took me a while to learn about prayer is that real prayer is so much more than just asking God for things."

"What do you mean?" Josh asked.

"Well, if the only time you and I talked was when you called up to ask me for something, what would happen?"

"You'd probably get sick of me calling," Josh laughed.

"Probably—even though I love you a lot. It's not that God gets sick of us asking Him for things, but He would like us to talk with Him at other times too."

"Like how?" Josh asked.

"When I was a kid in Sunday school my teacher wrote 'A C T S' on the board and asked us what it meant. I raised my hand and said that it was one of the books of the Bible—the book that explains how the early church got started. My teacher said, 'That's very good, Mr. Anderson, but now I would like you to develop a new understanding for "ACTS." ' My teacher then went on to say that we should use the word ACTS to guide our prayer lives. She explained that when we come to God in prayer we should A—adore Him; C—confess to Him; T—thank Him; and S—bring our supplication or our requests to Him. As I thought of my own prayer life, Josh, I realized that I spent most of my time in prayer 'supplicating'—asking God for stuff. Oh, I did some confession, too, and occasionally thanked Him, but I don't think I ever adored Him." Grandpa paused.

"Josh, have you ever told your mom and dad how much you love them?" Grandpa asked.

"Not recently, but I have."

"Have you ever told God how much you love Him?"

"Not really, but He must know that I do because He knows everything."

"I know that you love me, too, Josh, but it sure is nice to hear you say it."

Grandpa Anderson went on to explain to Josh the importance of having a set time each day for prayer. Before Josh left for the day, Grandpa and Josh bowed in prayer and Grandpa said, "Go ahead, Josh, tell God that you love Him."

Josh had never prayed aloud in front of anyone before, except when he said table grace or the Lord's Prayer, and so now, with his Grandpa waiting, he began rather hesitantly: "Dear God, I love You. I know that You died for me." Josh paused and looked up at his grandpa, who sat with his head bowed and a big smile on his face. Josh continued: "You know that I blow it sometimes; yet You don't stop loving me. I love You, too, God. I do. Amen." Josh looked up and saw a tear rolling down his Grandpa's cheek.

"That was beautiful, Josh," Grandpa said, before reaching over and rubbing Josh's head.

Finally, it was time to take Josh home. Grandpa Anderson made his way to the garage. Josh kissed his grandmother and thanked her *again for the delicious dinner—especially the homemade chocolate-chip cookies. His grandmother handed him a bag, "Here are the rest of the cookies to take home."*

"Thanks, Gram," Josh said, and then added, "I love you and Grandpa."

"We love you, too, dear." Grandma said.

Grandpa and Josh talked about hunting and fishing on the ride home. Pulling up in front of Josh's house, Grandpa asked, "Do you ever read that Bible that your grandmother and I gave you for your birthday?"

Josh smiled. "I've just started to."

Grandpa reached in his pocket and pulled out a piece of paper. "Here is a Bible passage that I'd like you to look up and maybe we can talk about it the next time we're together."

"Thanks, Grandpa," Josh said, reaching for the cookies beside him on the seat and the piece of paper with the Bible verse that his grandfather was handing to him. "I'll read it before I go to bed."

"Okay, Josh. Good-bye." Josh waved as his grandfather drove off.

Later that evening, Josh reached for the Bible that his grandparents had given him for his birthday and looked up the passage that his grandfather had written on the piece of paper. After a little searching, he found the verses:

And we ourselves know and believe the love which God has for us.

God is love, and whoever lives in love lives in union with God and God lives in union with Him. Love is made perfect in us in order that we may have courage on the Judgment Day; and we will have it because our life in this world is the same as Christ's. There is no fear in love; perfect love drives out all fear. So then, love has not been made perfect in anyone who is afraid, because fear has to do with punishment. We love because God first loved us. (1 John 4:16–19)

When Josh finished the passage, he closed the Bible. He remembered how his grandpa had taught him to pray. He started in, "Dear God, thanks for loving me first . . . "

Although Josh wasn't using this terminology, he was realizing that prayer is vital to developing the B part of his life.

Prayer is essential in allowing God's Spirit to guide us—in giving God the home-field advantage.

Learn

After Josh finished praying, he lay in bed, thinking about all that had happened. Adam and Brent had been avoiding him at school, and he had been avoiding them as well. His mom had asked him a couple more times what had happened, but he never came right out and told her. He thought about his grandparents and how wise they seemed to be. He thought about what his grandpa had taught him about prayer, and he wondered how his grandpa had gotten so smart.

As we seek to develop the B part of our lives, allowing God's Spirit to have control, we must learn all we can about God's will for our lives. How is this accomplished?

Josh had learned something special about his relationship with God when he read the passage his grandpa had written on the piece of paper. "We love because God first loved us" (1 John 4:19). Josh had occasionally pictured God as the "big policeman in the sky" who was always ready to arrest him and throw him in jail if he should happen to screw up. But now Josh was beginning to see God as someone who had made it possible for him to get out of jail—rather than seeing that he was locked up. Josh was falling madly in love with God.

How had Josh learned these things? What are some of the ways we learn about God's will for our lives? Let's mention some:

1. Through prayer. One of the most obvious ways that we learn about God's will is the way we just mentioned, through prayer. The more we talk with someone, the more we learn about him or her. (That's true most of the time!) It certainly is true with God. James 1:5 says, "But if any of you lacks wisdom, he should pray to God, who will give it to him; for God gives generously and graciously to all."

2. By reading and studying the Bible. Josh had learned something very important from reading the Bible. Josh had never really enjoyed reading the Bible before. He just did it once in a while because he felt that he had to do it. That's like trying to force someone to love you. But when he started reading the Bible willingly and with a positive attitude, he read more and he enjoyed it. Look at some of the things God says about the Bible:

> How can a young man keep his life pure?
>> By obeying Your commands.
>
> With all my heart I try to serve you;
>> keep me from disobeying Your
>>> commandments.
>
> I keep Your law in my heart,
>> so that I will not sin against You.
>
> I praise You, O Lord;
>> teach me Your ways.
>
> I will repeat aloud
>> all the laws You have given.
>
> I delight in following your commands
>> more than in having great wealth.

I study Your instructions;
> I examine Your teachings.
I take pleasure in Your laws;
> Your commands I will not forget.
Be good to me, Your servant,
> > so that I may live and obey Your
> > teachings.
Open my eyes, so that I may see
> the wonderful truths in Your law.
I am here on earth for just a little while;
> do not hide Your commands from me.
My heart aches with longing;
> > I want to know Your judgments at all
> > times.

> (Psalm 119:9–20)

Josh is beginning to see that the Bible is his source of power and his map, and his eyes are being opened to the wonderful promises and realities of God's Word: "Above all else, however, remember that no one can explain by himself a prophecy in the Scriptures. For no prophetic message ever came just from the will of man, but men were under the control of the Holy Spirit as they spoke the message that came from God" (2 Peter 1:20–21).

You see, the Bible differs from other books in that it was not written by people alone. God the Holy Spirit gave His chosen writers the thoughts they expressed and the words they used.

Like the passage from Psalms says, it is God's road map for our lives!

"All Scripture is inspired by God and is useful for teaching the truth, rebuking error, correcting faults, and giving instruction for right living, so that the person who serves God may be fully qualified and equipped to do every kind of good deed" (2 Timothy 3:16–17).

As Josh seeks to allow God's Spirit to control the B part of his life, and as we do the same, it is God's Word, the Bible, that has been given to us to show us God's plan of salvation and to teach us "right living."

Other books (like this one, for instance) that use the Bible as their basis for teaching can also be very valuable. Books like these, however, should never be read in place of the Bible, but always in addition to it.

3. By listening to God's Spirit. Jesus taught His disciples, "The Helper, the Holy Spirit, whom the Father will send in My name, will teach you everything and make you remember all that I have told you" (John 14:26).

In this verse we learn that the Holy Spirit provides comfort for us and will "teach [us] everything." God's Spirit is a great comfort and a great teacher.

When we get to the "Yield" in our acronym,

we will see how yielding to God's Spirit is the way to be taught by Him.

4. Through the fellowship of God's church. We learn a great deal about our relationship with God by sharing it with other believers. That's why we gather together—to learn through the fellowship of the family of believers. This would include all the teachers in the church as well. In Josh's case, his Grandpa Anderson, who is a part of the body of believers, has become one of the most important teachers in Josh's life.

God teaches us through Sunday school lessons, sermons, hymns, Scripture readings, prayer time, the church newsletter, Christian music, church missionaries, and all the other things we enjoy when God's family gets together. This is why the Bible says, "Let us not give up the habit of meeting together, as some are doing. Instead, let us encourage one another all the more, since you see that the Day of the Lord is coming nearer" (Hebrews 10:25).

Josh never realized all the ways God was speaking to him, trying to teach him, trying to help him learn. He is beginning to understand what it really means to P L A Y God's way!

Act

What would happen if Josh learned all about God's will for his life but never did anything about it? It would be sad, wouldn't it? To know what God wants you to do and not do it is sin.

Imagine the hottest summer day you've ever experienced. You are dying of thirst. Somebody

opens an ice-cold can of your favorite pop and hands it to you. "Here," they say, "quench your thirst." You grab the pop, hold it in your hand, but you never drink it. That would be stupid, wouldn't it?

That's the way lots of us are with God's Word. The Word teaches us about God's way. It teaches us that God's way quenches our thirst. Many learn it but never put it into action in their lives. They say they believe in God and have faith, but often times they don't live like it. James is blunt when he says, "You fool! Do you want to be shown that faith without actions is useless?" (James 2:20).

Learning more of God's Word means that we learn more about how we should live and act. We learn that we must spread His Word and be His witnesses. Acting on His Word will lead us down the path of service, of "loving our neighbors as ourselves." His Word tells us that others will know that we are followers of Christ by how we live and act.

The more Josh "learns" about how he should "act," the more he grows. He will learn the truth about God's forgiveness that is available when he yields to the bad spirit. He will learn how to confess his sins and practice the act of confession. His "acting" will lead Him into "yielding."

As Josh prays and learns more about God's

will for his life, it is most important that he does what God tells him to do. He must not only "hear" the word but "do" the word (James 1:22). How can you P L A Y if you never get off the bench?

Yield

It has been almost three weeks since Josh's argument with his friends. It has been uncomfortable avoiding them each day in school. His mother has asked him several more times about the argument with Adam and Brent, but Josh still hasn't wanted to talk about it. Whenever the subject comes up, Josh immediately feels a negative spirit. There is something inside him telling him to go to his friends and do whatever is necessary to win back their friendship, to be accepted by them. Something else tells him that he made the right decision, and that he has nothing to gain and lots to lose by giving in to his friends.

There is a war going on inside of Josh. Two very powerful forces are fighting to see to whom Josh will give control. It's like Galatians 5:16–17 says, "What I say is this: let the Spirit direct your lives, and you will not satisfy the desires of the human nature. For what our human nature wants is opposed to what the Spirit wants, and what the Spirit wants is opposed to what our human nature wants. These two are enemies, and this means that you cannot do what you want to do. If the Spirit leads you, then you are not subject to the Law."

Using our A B C model it looks like this:

 Josh is not communicating with his two best friends. They are at odds over his decision not to participate in their drinking and their watching of pornographic movies.

 The good spirit, the Holy Spirit, is telling Josh that being obedient to parents, to God's law, and being faithful to the pledge he made is more important than the relationship he had with his friends.

or

 The other force, the bad spirit, is telling Josh that he is being stupid. Every young person drinks once in a while. It's expected. And as far as porno flicks are concerned, hey, that's part of growing up. All parents expect their kids to experiment with stuff like this. It's natural.

 What Josh does.

What Josh does is going to be determined by which spirit gets the home-field advantage from Josh. The choice is his. If he gives the advantage to God's Spirit, the good spirit, he will stick to his guns and realize that he has made a decision pleasing to God. If, however, Josh gives the home-field advantage to the bad spirit, the devil, he will have decided that Adam and Brent's friendship is more important to him than doing what he knows in his heart is right. If he gives in to the bad spirit, he will be giving in to sin.

However, in the last three weeks there has been another war raging inside of Josh. Because of his conversations with his grandfather and the time he has spent reading the Bible and praying, he has become far more conscious of the role that God wants to play in His life. Using our model, Josh's thoughts look like this:

 God really loves me, and I love Him. He desires for me to learn more about Him and to spend more time with Him in prayer and in reading His Word. I've learned that God has a road map for me to follow.

Once again, the decision will be up to Josh as to which spirit he will award the home-field advantage:

 I am going to allow God's Spirit to guide me. I come to know God's will for my life through reading His Word and through prayer. I'm going to develop the same kind of relationship with Jesus that my grandparents have. I know that if my faith is really going to matter, I must not only know about God, I must follow His directions for my life.

or

I am going to go it on my own. I'm going to do it my way—the way most of the world does it. I'm not going to go overboard with this "religious stuff." I believe in God, so what? If He really loves me, He'll just let me do whatever I want to do.

Once again, C is going to be determined by whatever B—whatever spirit—Josh yields to. If Josh yields to the Spirit of God, the following will occur:

 God will richly bless his decision. Josh will grow and begin to experience the fruit of the Spirit: love, joy, peace, patience, kindness, goodness, faithfulness, humility, and self-control (Galatians 5:22–23). The problem with his friends might not be solved, and he might still feel uncomfortable, but he will have grown, and God promises that He rewards faithfulness.

If Josh yields to the evil spirit and does not allow the Spirit to rule his life, the following will occur:

 Josh will produce bad fruit. Among the bad fruit that marks the lives of people not controlled by God's Spirit are "immoral, filthy, and indecent actions; ... worship of idols and witchcraft. People become enemies and they fight; they become jealous, angry, and ambitious. They separate into parties and groups; they are envious, get drunk, have orgies, and do other things like these" (Galatians 5:19–21).

What decision will Josh make? If he is going to develop the B in his life, Josh will yield to the Spirit. Yielding is an essential part of P L A Y ing. You can't P L A without the Y.

It isn't easy for Josh. He wasn't aware of all that went in to being a follower of Jesus. Josh lifts weights in school and knows that building muscles takes lots of hard work. Weight lifting requires many hours of disciplined training. Josh is beginning to realize that being a follower of Jesus doesn't require many hours, it requires an entire life. Building up B requires *P* rayer, *L* earning, *A* cting and *Y* ielding. Is it worth it?

So, Who Are You?

Josh walked down the hall of Lincoln School. He entered his classroom and sat down. The bell rang, signaling the beginning of first hour. Mr. Larson, his teacher, said, "Good morning class, here are today's announcements." As Mr. Larson read the announcements, Josh glanced over at Adam, who was sitting on the opposite side of the room. He and Adam had not really communicated since their argument. Josh felt that his friendship with Adam was badly damaged, and he wished that they could be best friends again.

Josh kept looking at Adam, hoping that Adam would see him. Finally Adam did, and

Josh smiled at him and gave him a little wave. Adam smiled and waved back. Josh felt good.

Josh looked toward Mr. Larson just as he read the following announcement: "The Student Council is sponsoring a Valentine Dance next Friday night from 7 p.m. to 10 p.m. in the school cafeteria. The cost is $2. Get a date and come and dance to the music of the Lost Souls—Lincoln School's own top-forty rock band."

Josh's mind began to race with lots of thoughts: Adam smiled back . . . The Lost Souls . . . What a stupid name for a rock band . . . Those are the kids with earrings and motorcycle jackets . . . I wonder who I could go to the dance with . . . Who would want to go with me . . . Mr. Larson wears the same tie everyday . . . Adam smiled back . . . What about Brent . . . I wonder if Kari would go to the dance with me . . . I think she likes Paul.

Josh looked over at Paul. Paul is better looking than I am . . . Paul is more popular than I am . . . Paul is smarter than I am . . . Paul is a better basketball player than I am . . . Kari wouldn't go with me . . .

"All right, class. Let's go over the tests we took yesterday." Mr. Larson's loud voice derailed Josh's thoughts. "It is obvious that some of you are having trouble mastering algebra." Just as he said this, Mr. Larson laid Josh's test on his desk. Their eyes met. Josh looked at the grade on his test: F. A big, red F. And Mr. Larson had underlined it twice. Josh looked at the problems on the test. He hadn't gotten even one right. He knew he had done poorly, but he didn't think he had done this poorly.

Mr. Larson continued to hand back the tests. Josh felt flushed in the cheeks. As Mr. Larson handed Adam his test, he said, "Unless some of you start doing a lot better you are going to be repeating this class next year." Adam and Mr. Larson exchanged the same look Josh and Mr. Larson had. Josh thought: I bet Adam flunked the test too. And for some strange reason, that made Josh feel just a little better.

Josh had always gotten better grades than Adam. Josh knew that he was a better athlete than Adam. Josh also thought that he was better looking than Adam. Kari might not go to the dance with him, but she certainly wouldn't go with Adam. Adam's nose was weird, Josh thought, it looked like a banana. His mother had said that. People were always kidding Adam about his nose. Josh remembered one time when they were younger, he and Adam and Brent had argued about whose parents made the most money and whose father was the strongest. Ha! He couldn't remember who had won the argument. It didn't really matter now.

Kari, thought Josh. She is so pretty . . . So smart . . . She plays piano so well in choir . . . She dresses so nice . . . Paul . . . He likes Kari too . . . He's always the captain of the team . . . He always get A's . . . He sings the solos in choir . . . He doesn't have any zits like I do . . . I couldn't even ask Kari . . . I would die if she said no . . . I would die if she said yes . . . I can't ask her . . . She's probably going to go with Paul anyhow . . .

" . . . negative quantities are added by the subtraction of corresponding positive quantities . . . " Josh hadn't heard what Mr. Larson had said before this, his mind had been wandering, but this certainly didn't make any sense to him.

"What is this called?" Mr. Larson looked around the class. "Josh, what is this called?" Mr. Larson was talking to him.

Josh felt his face flush again, and finally answered: "I didn't hear what you said."

A few of the kids in the class giggled. Josh heard Adam's laugh among them.

"Paul, can you give us the answer?" Mr. Larson asked.

"The algebraic sum," Paul answered.

"Very good, Paul. Very good," Mr. Larson praised him.

Josh didn't think that the hour would ever come to an end. His day had started well, and

79

he was happy that Adam had waved back at him, but everything from that point on was a disaster. Once outside of class, Adam came up to Josh, punched him playfully, and said, "You better open your ears, Anderson!"

"Hi, Adam." And Josh felt his face flush again. Should he mention anything about their argument or not? Josh just looked at Adam's nose and smiled.

"Hey, what's so funny?" Adam asked.

"You. What grade did you get on the test?"

"I got a big fat F." Adam's voice emphasized the "F." Adam continued, "F as in . . . "

"Me too," Josh said bluntly, cutting Adam off.

"Really? I thought you did well in math?" Adam seemed surprised.

"I used to, but I just can't seem to understand algebra," Josh confessed.

"You got that right!" Adam agreed. "Hey, I'll catch you later."

"Catch you later, Adam."

As Josh stood at his locker, Kari walked by. Did she even know who he was? Did she even know that he was alive? Could he possibly get up enough courage to ask her to the dance?

What Josh is questioning is his self-worth. How good am I? What do others think of me? Am

I smart or stupid? Good looking or ugly? A good basketball player or a bad basketball player? A good friend or a bad friend? Someone others want to be around or someone others want to avoid? These are questions, or are similar to questions, that everyone asks themselves at some point in their lives. Let's look at them using our A B C model:

 There are thousands of situations that occur in our lives—hundreds every day. We must decide how we are going to accept and handle these situations.

In Josh's case, here are some of the situations he is facing:

 "Adam and I are talking again. I'm nuts about Kari, and I'm not sure she even knows I'm alive. I missed the free throw to tie the game last week. I got an F on my math test. Paul got the answer right. Paul probably got an A on his math test. I've got a couple of zits that are really ugly. God wants to be the most important person in my life."

Remember that there are two spiritual forces fighting for control in our lives. There is the good spirit, God's Spirit, and there is the evil spirit, the devil. Here is what happens if we give the home-field advantage to the bad spirit:

We start comparing ourselves with other people and use other people as our measuring stick. When we do this we never can be truly satisfied because there are always people who will be more successful than we are. We begin to feel inferior around others. We are more concerned about what others think, and what the world thinks, than we are about what God thinks. Bad fruit results, as explained in the last chapter. The following C occurs:

 We think of ourselves as we think others think of us. This will cause lots of heartache for us because very few other people really have our best interests in mind; consequently, they don't mind if we don't feel good about ourselves as long as they feel good about themselves.

The problem is that often we forget all about the B part of our lives. We go right from A to C. We need to stop after circumstances occur and evaluate our choices. This is where we then give God's Spirit the opportunity to guide us in His way. When we do, this is what happens:

 We examine all of the circumstances that happen to us in light of God's Word. We remember to P L A Y—pray, learn, act, yield. When we yield to God's Spirit in this area of our lives—in accepting ourselves as God has made us—we begin to enjoy peace of heart. Good fruit results. The following C occurs:

 We think of ourselves as God thinks of us. This is the "real you."

How does God see Josh? How does He see you and me?

Let's P L A Y.

First, we can *pray* and ask God what He thinks of us. Listen to His answer. In His Word, He'll tell you how much He loves you. I can hear Him talking to Josh, "Josh, I made you. You are unique. There is no one else in the world who has your fingerprints. You are one of a kind, Josh Anderson, and I need you to help others come to know Me and discover My love for them. I have a special plan just for you. Josh, I loved you so much that I allowed My Son to die in your place. I really love you, Josh."

Second, we can *learn* from God's Word what He tells us about the "real us." Look what David wrote:

> Lord, You have examined me and You know
>> me.
> You know everything I do;
>> from far away You understand all my
>> thoughts.
> You see me, whether I am working or
>> resting;
>> You know all my actions.
> Even before I speak,
>> You already know what I will say.
> You are all around me on every side;
>> You protect me with Your power.

Your knowledge of me is too deep;
> it is beyond my understanding.
Where could I go to escape from You?
> Where could I get away from Your
> presence?
If I went up to heaven, You would be there;
> if I lay down in the world of the dead,
> > You would be there.
If I flew away beyond the east
> or lived in the farthest place in the west,
You would be there to lead me,
> You would be there to help me.
I could ask the darkness to hide me
> or the light around me to turn into
> night,
but even darkness is not dark for You,
> and the night is as bright as the day.
> Darkness and light are the same to You.
You created every part of me;
> You put me together in my mother's
> womb.
I praise You because You are to be feared;
> all You do is strange and wonderful.
> I know it with all my heart.
When my bones were being formed,
> carefully put together in my mother's
> womb,
when I was growing there in secret,
> You knew that I was there—
> You saw me before I was born.
The days allotted to me

had all been recorded in Your book,
before any of them ever began.
O God, how difficult I find Your thoughts;
how many of them there are!
If I counted them, they would be more than
the grains of sand.
When I awake, I am still with You.
(Psalm 139:1–18)

Wow! Think of it! As Josh P L A Y s and grows and allows the Holy Spirit the home-field advantage in the B part of his life, he'll realize that the "real Josh" is this person God made who is so wonderfully complex and made by marvelous master workmanship.

Since Josh is a typical teenager, he is probably more concerned about what his friends think of him than he is about what God or his parents think of him. We are going to discuss these things in the following chapters. But if Josh's faith in Christ is going to mature, and if he is going to ACT and YIELD, he must understand who he is in God's eyes.

Who are you in Christ? What's your real identity? Look at what the Bible has to say about whose we are in Christ:

- YOU have been found "not guilty" of sin! *Romans 3:24*

- YOU are a brand new person!
  2 Corinthians 5:17

- YOU are now, through Jesus, the son
  (daughter) of God! *Ephesians 1:5–6*

- YOU are part of the family of God!
  Galatians 3:28

- YOU will be with Jesus forever!
  Ephesians 1:10–11

- YOU can approach God unafraid!
  Ephesians 3:12

- YOU have everything you need when you
  have Jesus! *Colossians 2:10*

Wow! That's how God sees YOU!

It is easy for Josh to worry about whether he is going to pass math, or go to the dance with Kari, or repair his friendship with Adam. He will wonder whether he is good looking, or smart, or accepted, but as his faith in Christ grows up as he grows up, Josh will learn to turn his thoughts more and more to who he is in Christ. That's from whom our real identity comes.

As Josh got off the bus and entered the house, his mother greeted him. "How was school, honey?"

"I flunked an algebra test," Josh answered, sharing at least a little of the turmoil of his day.

His mother seemed sympathetic and re-

plied, "I really struggled with algebra too. I never did quite understand that stuff. I think Mr. Larson passed me just so he wouldn't have me again the next year. And then to think I married an engineer. Maybe your dad could help you study."

"You had Mr. Larson too?" Josh was surprised.

His mother answered, "I think he's been there since they built the school." And she laughed.

"He always wears the same tie," Josh added, and laughed.

"It's probably the same one he wore when I had him," his mother joked.

"Wouldn't doubt it," Josh said, heading to his room. As he opened the door of his bedroom, he noticed the Bible from his grandpa sitting on his dresser. Learn, he thought. Learn. He picked the Bible up and walked over to his bed. It felt good to lie down after the day he'd had. He opened up the Bible and then shut it, deciding to spend a few minutes in prayer. He wanted to talk to God about who he was and whether he mattered much. He wanted to talk to God about algebra and Adam and freethrows and test scores. And he wanted to talk to God about Kari.

So, What about the Family?

Josh was right. Kari was going to the dance with Paul. Josh had learned this right at the end of basketball practice after school. It was all he thought about as he rode the late bus home.

Josh entered the house. His mother greeted .him: "How was school today, honey?"

"Fine," Josh answered.

"Anything exciting happen today?" his mother asked.

"No."

"How was basketball?" His mother always asked the same questions.

"Fine," Josh answered.

"Do you have lots of homework tonight?" Another typical question of his mother's.

"Some," Josh answered, as he walked down the hallway to his room, passing his sister Kendra's room. Kendra was two years older than Josh. Josh looked into her room: There she sat, studying again. She was always studying. And look at her room—not a thing out of place. Josh couldn't even guess what wonders he had hiding under the bed in his room.

Kendra heard Josh and turned to him. "I heard you're flunking algebra." She said it as though she had been happy to hear about it.

"I'm not flunking the whole class, I just had a bad test," Josh defended himself.

"That's not what I heard," Kendra said with a smile.

"Who told you about it, anyhow?" Josh questioned.

"Mom said that you were flunking Mr. Larson's class and asked me if I could help you," Kendra said.

Josh stormed downstairs to find his mother. He found her in the kitchen and immediately questioned her, "Why did you tell Kendra that I was flunking Mr. Larson's class?"

"I didn't tell her that," his mother answered, and she was just about to continue when Josh interrupted:

"That's what she said." There was fire in Josh's eyes.

"I told her you had failed a test and were having trouble. I thought maybe she could help you study." His mom tried to calm him.

She wasn't successful, and Josh became even more irritated as he yelled: "I need her help like I need a hole in my head! If I need anybody's help, I'll ask for it. You had no business telling her about my grades. I guess I can't trust you to tell you about anything! Why don't you call up Grandma and Grandpa and tell them too! Better yet, why don't you put it on CNN!"

"Josh, don't you talk to me like that! I was trying to help you." Now his mother was angry.

"I don't need any help!" Josh yelled again as he stormed up the stairs to his room.

His mother followed him. Kendra walked to the door of her room and positioned herself in a good spot to watch the show.

Josh's mother tried to enter his room, but the door was locked. She yelled, "Josh, open this door right now! I want to talk with you!"

There was a moment of silence, followed by a loud blast of rock music from inside the room.

"Josh, open this door instantly or you are going to be grounded for a month!" his mother threatened.

Although Josh didn't think his mother was

serious, he knew that he was going to have to open the door sooner or later, so reluctantly he opened the door. His mother charged in, walked over to his stereo, and turned off the music. She stood for a moment near Josh where he lay on the bed before expressing her anger. "Look at this room! It looks like a tornado hit it! I work all day long, and I just don't have the energy to come home and pick up after you!"

Josh answered, "It's my room. If you don't like it, you don't have to come in it."

"Watch it, boy! You are walking on thin ice! Who do you think does the laundry? Who buys these clothes you leave lying all around? Who does the ironing and the vacuuming?"

Josh figured that his mother didn't really expect any answers to these questions. It wasn't the first time he had heard her ask them, and he knew that it probably wasn't going to be the last either.

She continued: "It's about time you start taking some of the responsibility around here. This isn't a hotel. We're a family, and everyone has to pull their share of the weight."

Mother walked over to the closet and slid open the door. "Look at this crap! How can you live in such a mess? Doesn't it bother you to live like this?"

Josh answered, "You should see Adam's room."

"We're not talking about Adam! We're talking about your room!" His mother was red in the cheeks.

"I thought we were talking about why you told Kendra about my flunking an algebra test!" Josh was still angry too. "How did the subject get changed to my room? It's been like this for weeks. Why start yelling at me about it now? I get so sick and tired of you and Dad always comparing me with Kendra. It makes me sick! I hate it! I hate it!" Now Josh was almost to the point of tears. His mother stood silent for a moment.

Josh continued, "My grades are never as good as Kendra's. My room is never as clean as Kendra's. Why can't I help around the house more—like Kendra does. Why don't I like to play the piano—like Kendra does. Kendra always remembers your birthday and your anniversary. God, I wish I could be perfect like Kendra!"

"Josh, that's unfair. We don't love Kendra more than we love you. We love you both the same." His mother meant it.

Josh was quick to answer, "I didn't say that you loved her more. Open your ears! I said that I hate it when you are always comparing me

93

with her. Why can't you just accept me the way that I am?"

Sound at all familiar? Family conflict. No family is free from it. It happens in even the best of families. Some families become so torn apart by it that communication between family members ceases completely. Some brothers and sisters spend their entire lives being bitter with one another. Some take their bitterness to the grave. Some children never get over the hurt that was caused them by their parents. Some parents never get over the hurt caused them by their children. This certainly isn't the way that God intended families to be. So why is it that these conflicts occur?

We can see it in our A B C model:

 Situations occur in the family. These situations will test the family's relationships. The family will either grow together or grow apart depending on

 How they choose to handle the situations. There are two possible alternatives. They can handle the situation God's way or the devil's way. To whom will they give the home-field advantage?

The following B and C result when family members give the home-field advantage to the bad spirit:

If they give the home-field advantage to the evil spirit, they will be looking at the situations from a self-centered point of view. Their emphasis will be on "me." "What is best for me?" "What do I want?" This is not God's way. If the family does this, the following results:

 There will be continued discord in the family. The family might even be destroyed.

Using the same A, the following B and C result when family members give the home-field advantage to God's spirit:

 The family looks at the situations from God's point of view. The emphasis is off "self," and family members think in terms of how they can be servants rather than how they can be served. This will work for you even if the other members of the family do not share your faith. If you yield to God's Spirit, the following results:

 You cannot change your family, but you can change yourself. The neat thing is that often when one member of the family changes, it has an impact on the rest of the family. If you start doing things God's way, He has promised you that good will result from it. That's a sure promise! In the very least, you will start seeing situations (the A's) differently and will handle them differently (the B's) and this is going to dramatically change your C's—what you do!

Okay. Being a Christian means doing things God's way. Being a Christian means seeing things as God sees them. The family is one of the major battle grounds where our faith is either going to work or not work. If we live like Christians at home, there will be results. What is God's point of view for the family? How would the story about Josh and his mother have changed if things had been done God's way? Let's go to the A B C model again:

 Situations occur. Look at the situation as each of the characters in our story saw it:

In Josh's case, he was depressed that Kari was going to the dance with Paul. He was tired after a hard basketball practice, and Adam had seemed real strange when he had tried to talk to him in the hall after first hour class. Algebra wasn't getting any easier, and the possibility of flunking the class suddenly seemed very real. The last thing in the world he needed was to be harassed by his sister and yelled at by his mother about his messy room.

In his mother's case, she had had a hard day at work. She worked at the bank and had spent half the day looking for a major error made on a deposit slip. Her boss was angry and was taking it out on all the employees. She had come home to find that the hamburger she had wanted to have for supper was still in the freezer. Then she had walked into the laundry room to see a big pile of clothes lying on the floor where Josh had dumped them. Her husband had called to say that he was going to happy hour at a local bar with some clients, and that he was going to be late for supper. She had wondered how her husband would have felt if she had called him to tell him that she was going to happy hour with a bunch of friends. She wondered why supper was always her responsibility, and the laundry, and the vacuuming, and the house cleaning. She was happy to see Josh get home. At times she still thinks of him as "her little boy." She would have just loved a hug from him, but instead, he had hardly even talked to her, and had answered her questions with one-word responses. She felt that the time had come for her to get some of the respect she deserved.

In Kendra's case, she thinks Josh gets away with murder. He rarely studies. His room is a mess. He was allowed to quit piano lessons. He gets to do things that she never did at his age. Her parents are always talking to her about boys, and although they don't come right out and say it, she thinks they are worried about her getting pregnant. They never seem to worry about Josh and who he hangs out with. If they knew some of the things that she has heard about Adam and Brent and the things they do . . . She gets real tired of always being perfect. Just once she would like to leave her room a mess. Just once she wished no one would expect her to always get good grades. She thinks Josh is more normal than she is. He seems more accepted by other kids in school. Why does she have to be so different?

Isn't it strange? The same situation viewed in three totally different ways. Add father's point of view and other children's—if the family had them—and suddenly you get the picture: The family is a group of human beings who all see things from different points of view. The secret to family harmony is to have everyone in the family pulling in the same direction, rather than everyone pulling in their own direction. In the following chapter we'll see how, as followers of Christ, we can have His eyes and see things as He sees them.

So, You Want to Have Your Father's Eyes?

I'll never forget my first car. My grandfather left it to me in his will. It was a 1954 Buick Special. My grandfather had taken excellent care of the car, and when he died in 1970 it only had 30,000 miles on it. I had spent quite a few Saturdays at my grandparents' house, and I used to earn some money helping around their yard. One of the chores I enjoyed the most was helping wash and wax Grandpa's car. He called the car "Betty." I'll never forget the first time I drove Betty out of Grandpa's garage and drove it to my house. It was

now my car, but it was also a symbol to me of my grandparents' love.

I drove Betty until it could be driven no more. The bottom was rusted out and the engine was in danger of falling out of the car. But I haven't had the heart to have Betty junked. I still have her and spend money every month to rent a garage where I keep her. Someday, I keep telling myself, I'm going to be able to afford to have Betty fixed up as good as new. But now she sits in the garage, badly rusted from the road salt of many Minnesota winters. Her paint is faded and flaky from too many hot summers. The taillights are broken. The tires are flat. The steering wheel is cracked. But I still love Betty. I can still see Grandma and Grandpa pulling up in front of our house in Betty. Grandpa gets out of the car and walks around to the passenger side and opens the door for Grandma. He holds out his arm for her as they walk up the steps of our sidewalk toward our house. That's what I see when I look at my car.

If you looked at the car you would see an old wreck ready for the junkyard. And we are looking at the same car.

How you see things is called "perception." You may see the exact same thing someone else sees and yet see something totally different. I heard a speaker once who said "No two people ever see the same sunset." I thought a lot about that. What did he mean?

You see, to one person the sunset might mean romance. To a person dying of cancer who has been told that he only has a month to live, the sunset might mean that the end is that much nearer. To a golf course attendant the sunset may mean the end of another day of work.

This is so important to understand. Understanding perception will change the way you see the real you. It will affect the way you communicate and act as part of the family. It will dramatically change how you relate with your peers. You see, you are all seeing the same things but you are seeing them with your individual eyes.

What is it that causes us to see the same things so differently than others? Good question. If we both looked at Betty, why would we see something so completely different? Three things determine your perception:

1. Your values. How you see things is determined to a large degree by what you value. Value is basically the worth or importance you attach to things. The more value you attach to something, the more important it becomes to you. This, of course, then affects the way you see things. What might seem important to you may not mean anything to someone else.

For instance, you probably wouldn't be too

thrilled if I gave you Betty. She would be a burden for you. You'd have to spend thousands and thousands of dollars to fix her up. It wouldn't be worth it to you. However, I wouldn't let you have Betty, even if you offered me $5,000 for her.

If you value popularity, you'll probably be disappointed if you're not chosen as one of the leaders of your class. If you value money, you'll look for opportunities to gain it. The amount of value you place on it will determine the amount of time you spend earning it or gaining it. If you value acceptance by peers, you might act in such a way as to be accepted: Dress the right way, say the right things, etc. If you value your family, you'll work on building family togetherness and realize the importance of spending time together.

We can see how the values we have help color the way we see—or perceive—things.

2. Your attitude. Yeah, you've heard a lot about your attitude. One popular speaker said: "It's not your aptitude but your attitude that determines your altitude!" Clever. And true. So what is it about attitude, anyhow? Well, attitude is at the heart of how we perceive things. Look at this story that Jesus told:

> A teacher of the Law came up and tried to trap Jesus. "Teacher," he asked, "what must I do to receive eternal life?"

Jesus answered him. "What do the Scriptures say? How do you interpret them?"

The man answered, " 'Love the Lord your God with all your heart, with all your soul, with all your strength, and with all your mind'; and 'Love your neighbor as you love yourself.' "

"You are right," Jesus replied; "do this and you will live."

But the teacher of the Law wanted to justify himself, so he asked Jesus, "Who is my neighbor?"

Jesus answered, "There was once a man who was going down from Jerusalem to Jericho when robbers attacked him, stripped him, and beat him up, leaving him half dead.

"It so happened that a priest was going down that road; but when he saw the man, he walked on by on the other side. In the same way a Levite also came there, went over and looked at the man, and then walked on by on the other side. But a Samaritan who was traveling that way came upon the man, and when he saw him, his heart was filled with pity. He went over to him, poured oil and wine on his wounds and bandaged them; then he put the man on his own animal and took him to an inn, where he took care of him. The next day he took out two silver coins and gave them to the innkeeper. 'Take care of him,' he told the innkeeper, 'and when I come back this way, I will pay you whatever else you spend on him.' "

And Jesus concluded, "In your opinion, which one of these three acted like a neighbor toward the man attacked by the robbers?"

The teacher of the Law answered, "The one who was kind to him."

Jesus replied, "You go, then, and do the same." (Luke 10:25–37)

Think about the story for a minute. Can you see how each person in the story viewed the beaten man differently? The bandits who robbed the man and beat him and left him beside the road saw him as vulnerable prey, ripe for the taking. The priest and the Levite saw him as a burden to themselves. Both went out of their way to avoid him. The Samaritan saw the poor man as someone desperately in need of help, someone, who because of his need, was his neighbor. Each person perceived the man differently because they had different values, attitudes, and needs. How do you think Jesus views all of the characters in the story? How does Jesus view you?

You see how your attitude also determines how you see—how you perceive circumstances and situations. In fact, your attitude will determine how you see yourself and how you see others. Sinful behavior begins with the wrong attitude. Being a Christian and giving God the home-field advantage in the B part of our lives where our decisions are made, means developing a godly attitude—seeing things like Jesus sees them and then responding as Jesus would respond.

Knowing that Jesus loves us immeasurably, and sees us as His children, helps us keep a positive attitude, and helps us respond to others as brothers and sisters. Check out these words of Paul from his letter to the Philippians:

> May you always be joyful in your union with the Lord. I say it again: rejoice!
>
> Show a gentle attitude toward everyone. The Lord is coming soon. Don't worry about anything, but in all your prayers ask God for what you need, always asking Him with a thankful heart. And God's peace, which is far beyond human understanding, will keep your hearts and minds safe in union with Christ Jesus.
>
> In conclusion, my brothers, fill your minds with those things that are good and that deserve praise: things that are true, noble, right, pure, lovely, and honorable. Put into practice what you learned and received from me, both from my words and from my actions. And the God who gives us peace will be with you." (4:4–8)

I remember when I was a child, I heard someone say that an optimist is someone who looks at a carton of milk and says, "The carton is half-full." A pessimist is someone who looks at the same carton and says, "The carton is half-empty." Well, a Christian is someone who looks at things with the eyes of Jesus and sees them as Jesus would see them. This is what Paul asks of his friends and fellow believers in Philippi: "Fill your minds with those things that are good and that deserve praise: things that are true, noble, right, pure, lovely, and honorable." Excellent advice concerning our attitude!

Stop for a moment right now and think about your values and your attitude. Are your values in keeping with Christ's values? Do you try to see things with Jesus' eyes? Do you fix your thoughts on what is true and good and right? The choice is up to you. Here is another area where the spirits do battle. Has God led you to give His Spirit the home-field advantage? If so, think of how your values and attitudes have changed. How does this affect your relationship with yourself and your relationship with your family?

If you haven't been giving God's Spirit the advantage, stop and talk to Him now. He loves you so much that He sent His Son to die for you. He stands ready to forgive you and renew you with His Spirit's power.

3. Your needs. The other major players in determining how you perceive things are your needs. The more you need something the more value you attach to it and the more it affects your attitude concerning it. For example, if I am very sick with a fever, I will value medicine that will help take my fever away. If I don't have a fever, however, I don't even think about the need for medicine.

Just a few days ago a very dirty, poorly dressed man came up to me on the street and asked me for a quarter to help pay for bus fare home. A quarter seemed like a very small sum to me, but it meant a lot to the man. Once again, two people are looking at the same thing and seeing something differently. One of the reasons we perceive it differently is because of our need for it.

What needs do you have? We all have basic needs: food, shelter, and clothing. Most of us don't even think of needing these things because we've never been without them. That's not the way it is in much of the world, however. In Cairo, Egypt, for instance, more than 10,000 people earn a living by sorting through garbage in the city's dump. They are lucky to make 50 cents a day. They actually live in among the garbage in huts made out of tin and cardboard and cloth. There is no clean water. Rats infest the huts and carry diseases. Each day 10–15 children die. Those who live are malnourished and are often covered with sores. Tell these people about your need for a room of your own. Tell these people about your need for your own telephone. Tell these people how you are going to need your own car. Tell these people about your need for a new video game.

You see how need determines how you perceive things? What, really, are your needs? I don't mean to go on and on about it, but honestly, your relationship with your family, with yourself, with others, and your relationship with God is ultimately going to be determined by what you think you need. Well, what do you need? Beyond the needs of food, shelter, and clothing I believe that another basic human need is the need to be loved. We all want to be loved. For most of us, the need to be loved is met in and through our families. But human love alone can't fill the area of our lives that is made empty because of our sinful nature. Only God's Spirit can fill that emptiness.

We all experience the need to have that emptiness filled. We attempt to fill the need in lots of different ways: We accumulate things (materialism); we look for it in members of the opposite sex (premarital sex; extramarital sex); some look for it with members of the same sex (homosexuality); we experiment with alcohol and drugs (substance abuse); we try to entertain ourselves so we don't have to think about our needs (television, movies, music, books, sports, play, etc.); we work hard to try to rise to the top (power and work addiction); we dress the way others do and talk the way others do to try to find acceptance (peer pressure). Oh, we try lots of different things to try to fill the need we have for love, but there is only one way that need can really be met: By having a close, personal relationship with Jesus Christ.

You see, that's where Josh Anderson is in his life. Jesus is beginning to become real to him. Jesus is becoming more than just somebody to sing about. Jesus is becoming Josh's best friend. Jesus wants to be your best friend too. When Jesus becomes your best friend, you examine your needs in the light of His Word. This changes your perception of things. You realize that what you need is not to be served, but to be a servant.

Values, attitudes, and needs: The three things that determine how you perceive things, situations, people. When you are a Christian, you perceive things as Christ would. This means that the choices you face are perceived differently too. You desire to be a servant rather than to be served. You face mountains—problems and trials that come your way—and you move ahead in confidence. You operate by faith rather than by feelings. You look to God and His Word for direction, rather than to the opinion of friends.

As Josh grows—as you grow in the faith— you'll start to look at things with your Father's eyes and with your Father's heart! If you take your faith seriously, it is bound to affect how you relate in your family—how you get along with Mom and Dad and that brother or sister.

So, How Can I Apply My Faith at Home?

If being a Christian means seeing things with God's eyes, how does that affect the way you relate with your family? When you develop a mature faith—a faith that works—the way you see many circumstances and the way you behave are bound to change.

Remember the A B C's? When you allow God to control the B area of your life and give His Spirit the home-field advantage, you will even begin to perceive A differently.

Back to our story about Josh:

113

Mom spoke, "Josh, I love you, and I want you to do well in school. I thought you've seemed down lately—ever since you came home from Adam's a few weeks ago. I thought maybe the trouble you were having with algebra was also causing you to be depressed. I mentioned your grade to Kendra because I thought she could help you. I didn't mean to embarrass you. But you mustn't talk to me the way you did. I'm your mother, Josh, and you shouldn't talk to me like that. You shouldn't talk to anyone like that. Now get up off the bed and clean this room." His mother exited, shutting the door behind her.

Josh lay without moving for a few minutes. He heard the telephone ring. After a moment Kendra opened the door to his room: "There's a telephone call for you," she said, "I think it is Adam." Josh quickly ran to the phone in his parents' room.

"I've got it, you can hang up now," Josh yelled. "Hi, Adam." Josh answered, happy that his friend had called.

"Hi, Josh." Adam's voice sounded weird.

"What's wrong?" Josh asked.

"My parents are getting a divorce. My dad has left home and is staying at some motel." Josh could tell now that Adam was crying.

"Oh, no." Josh really felt for his friend. "Maybe they will get back together," Josh said, trying to find some hope. "Maybe after a few days things will get better."

"I think this time they mean it. They've been arguing and talking about divorce for the last few years. I told them once that if they got divorced that I would kill myself . . ." Adam broke off, trying hard not to let Josh know how much he was crying.

"Don't be stupid," Josh said, saying the first thing that came to his mind. Then he remembered what one of his teacher's had said about suicide—always take a threat seriously. "Listen, Adam, why don't you come over and we'll talk."

Adam continued, "My dad was drunk and said that if I killed myself he wasn't going to pay for the funeral." Adam didn't even try to hold back the tears now.

There were a few minutes of silence. Finally, Josh said, "Gosh, I'm sorry, Adam. I didn't know your folks didn't get along."

"Sometimes I think that if I were dead they'd get along better. My mother is always talking about how much I cost them and how I'm a burden to them."

Josh renewed his earlier offer, taking Adam's threat seriously, "Adam, come on over and have dinner with us. I'm sure it will be okay with Mom."

"Are you sure?" Adam asked.

"Yeah, Mom will understand," Josh said, suddenly having a different perception of his family.

"I'll see you in about 15 minutes. Bye," Adam said, hanging up.

"Bye," Josh said before Adam had hung up the phone. Josh put down the receiver and sat for a moment on his parents' bed. He thought, *Poor Adam. What can I do to help?* The only thing he could think of doing he had already done when he invited Adam for dinner. All of a sudden, Josh had another idea: He bowed his head and said a prayer for Adam. And then he prayed for Adam's dad. And then he prayed for Adam's mom. And then he thanked God for his family. Somehow he felt strangely better after talking things over with God.

After he finished praying, Josh went down to the kitchen where his mother was. He told her about Adam and the situation with Adam's parents. His mother was happy that he had invited Adam to dinner. Josh looked at his mom for a moment, and then said, "Mom, I'm sorry that I talked to you the way I did. I've had a really rotten day. I didn't mean to take it out on you. Please forgive me."

"You're forgiven." His mother's response was quick, and then she added with a smile,

"Now show me that you are sincere by trying to clean up your room at least a little before Adam gets here."

"Mom," Josh said, the tone of his voice communicating his feelings as he headed up to his room. He picked up a pair of shorts from the floor and was folding them up to put them back in a drawer when he saw the Bible from his grandparents on his dresser. He remembered what his Grandpa wrote in the inside cover: "This book will keep you from sin, or sin will keep you from this book." Josh made a vow to read a chapter or two before he went to bed.

Josh and Adam are two normal teenagers. There is one big difference between the two, however. The difference has nothing to do with their parents, or their looks, or their intelligence, the difference has to do with the way they respond to God's Spirit. God is becoming a very important player in Josh's life. If you asked Adam, he would tell you that he believes in God, but God doesn't really make a difference in his life. This is the choice the Holy Spirit is waiting to help us all make: To what degree are we going to get involved with God? It doesn't matter if we live in a happy family or a dysfunctional family. It doesn't matter whether we live in a mansion or in a garbage dump. What are you going to do with Jesus?

If, like Josh, you desire to have Jesus as your

number-one player, then as you develop the B of your life, and remember to P L A Y, Jesus has some instructions for you concerning your role in the family. Let's look at some of them:

1. Exodus 20:12. "Respect your father and your mother, so that you may live a long time in the land that I am giving you." This is one of the Ten Commandments. It requires children to honor their parents even if they think their parents don't honor them. It is called "the first commandment with a promise." Someone a long time ago said, "As the home goes so goes the nation." There is so much truth to that saying. If parents are honorable and honor their children, and if children return that honor to their parents, and together God is honored, there will be happy homes and happy lives.

This is God's design for families. But we know that this is a picture we won't always see on earth. More than likely, there are times when you are not happy and when your home is not happy. When you have times like that, remember that God stands ready to help you.

2. Romans 1:29–30. "They are filled with all kinds of wickedness . . . . They gossip and speak evil of one another; they are hateful to God, insolent, proud, and boastful; they think of more ways to do evil; they disobey their parents." This is part of Paul's description of people who allow the bad spirit to control the B part of their lives. Satan could not find a better way to attack us than to do it through our families. Family relationships crumble when some in the family are more concerned about their individual rights than they are about what is best for the family.

3. Colossians 3:14—21. The Bible puts down some important rules for relationships in the family:

> And to all of these qualities add love, which binds all things together in perfect unity. The peace that Christ gives is to guide you in the decisions you make; for it is to this peace that God has called you together in the one body. And be thankful. Christ's message in all its richness must live in your hearts. Teach and instruct one another with all wisdom. Sing psalms, hymns, and sacred songs; sing to God with thanksgiving in your hearts. Everything you do or say, then, should be done in the name of the Lord Jesus, as you give thanks through Him to God the Father.
>
> Wives, submit yourselves to your husbands, for that is what you should do as Christians. Husbands, love your wives and do not be harsh with them.
>
> Children, it is your Christian duty to obey your parents always, for that is what pleases God.

Parents, do not irritate your children, or they will become discouraged. (Colossians 3:14–21).

Again, this is God's design for families. What if your parents aren't Christians? Always remember that you cannot change other people. You are responsible for how you relate with God. If your parents aren't Christians and you are, let them see that your faith is real. How can you do that? Well, by obeying Scripture. By honoring them and finding ways to show Christ's love to them. You should do this, of course, when your parents are Christians too.

4. Check these verses out: "Children, it is your Christian duty to obey your parents, for this is the right thing to do. 'Respect your father and mother' is the first commandment that has a promise added: 'so that all may go well with you, and you may live a long time in the land' " (Ephesians 6:1–3).

I remember as a kid that I thought my parents were very unreasonable at times. One of my dad's favorite things was to compare how easy I had it compared with how tough it was for him as a kid—the old, "Back when I was a kid we had to walk to school barefoot in the snow, 25 miles uphill both ways" routine. Now that I'm a parent and have four children of my own, I perceive things a little differently. I realize that sometimes parents live out their lives through their kids. They want their children to succeed where they may have failed. Parents become overprotective. (My wife and I have agreed that we WILL allow our children to date—when they turn 35—but only then if one us of accompanies them!)

Try to see things from your parents' point of view. Remember the old Indian saying: "Don't criticize someone until you've walked a mile in his moccasins." Some day when you are a parent yourself, you will probably hear yourself say those same things you heard your parents say that you promised yourself you'd never say if you lived to be a thousand years old. Trust me on this. You will.

Accept the fact that your parents are human too. No, they won't always be fair. Sometimes they may not understand. But always remember they have needs and expectations just like you do. And so do your brothers and sisters. Ask yourself these questions: What would Jesus do? Would Jesus be a tattletale? Would Jesus gossip? Does it make Jesus happy to see other people fail? Try to relate to the rest of your family in this manner. You'll notice significant changes—if not in them—in you!

There have been entire books written on this subject, but let me offer just a few valuable suggestions as to how your family can give God's Spirit the home-field advantage:

1. Talk with each other. It's amazing how little we talk anymore. Often times, even when we are together, we have a television on or music playing. Communicating with one another requires discipline, and in our fast-paced society it isn't easy, but talk to your parents about having a special time set aside when you can just talk. It might have to begin with talking about talking.

Then: Watch your talk! Unfortunately, much of the talk that does occur in families is negative. There are often put-downs, and things are said without thinking. It is very important that you watch what you say and how you say it. Words can destroy tender spirits. The Bible says, "Patient persuasion can break down the strongest resistance" (Proverbs 25:15). I love this one, also from Proverbs: "The more you talk, the more likely you are to sin. If you are wise, you will keep quiet" (Proverbs 10:19).

Obviously, there are times when you have to listen. When you do listen, really try to hear what the other person is saying. Don't rush to figure how you should answer. Listen! Identify the feelings behind what is being said. Acknowledge the other person's feelings.

The tongue can cause a lot of trouble unless

it is watched. Look what James says about the tongue:

> My brothers, not many of you should become teachers. As you know, we teachers will be judged with greater strictness than others. All of us often make mistakes. But if a person never makes a mistake in what he says, he is perfect and is also able to control his whole being. We put a bit into the mouth of the horse to make it obey us, and we are able to make it go where we want. Or think of a ship: big as it is and driven by such strong winds, it can be steered by a very small rudder, and it goes wherever the pilot wants it to go. So it is with the tongue: small as it is, it can boast about great things.
>
> Just think how large a forest can be set on fire by a tiny flame! And the tongue is like a fire. It is a world of wrong, occupying its place in our bodies and spreading evil through our whole being. It sets on fire the entire course of our existence with the fire that comes to it from hell itself.
>
> (James 3:1–6)

It is essential that you talk. It is also essential that you listen. Never forget the importance of the tongue—what is said and *how* it is said can either build something up or tear something down. Jesus always built others up with what He said. He set a good example for us.

2. Worship together and set aside time other than your regular church time when your family gets together for devotions and prayer. Some people call this "the family altar." It isn't a real altar like you have in church, but it is a time when the family gets together to share from His Word and pray together. You will need to talk with your parents about this if you don't already do it. Be prepared! So few families actually do this, that the idea is quite foreign. But the old saying is so true: "The family that prays together, stays together!" How about once a week—maybe Sunday afternoon after lunch—sitting down together for a devotion and prayer? Turn off the television. Take the phone off the hook. Fellowship with the most important people in your life!

Of course, you should have your own personal "altar" as well—that special place and time where you feel close to God and communicate with Him.

These times of family and personal devotions really strengthen your faith and make it work. As you come together as a family to share your faith, you also share your hurts and joys. You can be honest about your fears. During this time you can confess your sins and reaffirm God's forgiveness. This time will do so much to bring your family closer together and closer to God.

If others in your family are not interested in

establishing regular family altar time, perhaps you can find a friend or two—members of your youth group at church—or grandparents or other trusted adults, who will share a devotional time with you on a regular basis.

Your faith will really grow as you study God's Word and talk to Him in prayer.

3. Act and yield. Remember our P L A Y acronym for giving God's Spirit the edge? Well, we *pray* and *learn* about how God wants us to act in the family; it then becomes essential that we *act* and *yield* the way He wants us to. We learn that God wants us to be His servants. How can we do that in the family? Here are a few suggestions:

a. The next time you are about to talk back to your parents, button your lip—or listen and do what they say without arguing.

b. The next time you are about to put down a brother or sister, button your lip—or find something positive to say instead. Then go to your room and say a prayer for them.

c. Look for jobs that need to be done around the house and do them without being asked. Is there garbage that needs taking out? A room (probably yours) that needs to be cleaned? A yard that could be mowed? A sidewalk that could be shoveled? (For those of us who live in tundra country!) Laundry that could be washed? Windows that could be cleaned? You get the idea. Find some jobs that need to be done and do them without being asked. Your parents will wonder what you're up to.

d. The next time your family is going to go out and eat, tell your parents that you'll be happy with whatever place they pick. No, you don't need pizza again!

e. Really do something freaky and make your sister or brother's bed while they are in the shower.

f. Serve your parents breakfast in bed. (Don't dump it on them!)

These are only a few suggestions. What others can you come up with? You see, servanthood begins at home. Even if you are an orphan you are part of God's family, and we show our love for one another in the way that we serve one another. The really amazing things is—are you ready for this—the more love you give away the more you receive in return. Try it in your family and experience it for yourself.

There are two promises to remember concerning your family and the things that happen to you in your life. When things seem bleak, and it may seem impossible to be a Christian at home, remember this promise: "I have the strength to face all conditions by the power that Christ gives me" (Philippians 4:13).

And when things don't turn out the way you think they should, remember this promise: "We know that in all things God works for good with those who love Him, those whom He has called according to His purpose" (Romans 8:28).

Now, back to Josh.

About 15 minutes after Josh had finished talking to Adam on the phone—just like Adam said—he rang the doorbell at Josh's house. "I'll get it," Josh yelled from his room, where he was busy picking up clothes from under his bed and throwing them in a basket to take to the laundry room downstairs. "It's probably Adam."

Josh ran to the front door. It was Adam, his eyes red from crying. "Come in, buddy," Josh said, somewhat at a loss for words.

Mrs. Anderson came to greet Adam as well. She looked at his swollen eyes and put her arm around his shoulder. "I'm really sorry to hear about your parents, Adam. I'm praying that everything will be all right."

Josh looked at his mother with her arm around Adam. Adam began to cry. There were tears in his mother's eyes, and Josh tried to hold back the tears in his own eyes. Josh stared at his mom. He felt mighty proud that she was his mother.

So, What about the Rest of the World?

Dinner went well. After discovering that the hamburger wasn't thawed and that her husband was going to be late, Mrs. Anderson had ordered out for pizza—Josh's favorite meal. Adam ate more than his share, and Josh was happy to see that he still had an appetite.

Josh was surprised, too, that during the meal Kendra seemed almost nice to him and Adam. She hadn't made one put-down. Josh wondered if it maybe had something to do with his prayer. It had been his turn to pray before the meal, and instead of reciting the same memorized table grace he usually did, he said a prayer in his own words. He thanked God for the day, and for his family, and then he asked God to be with Adam and his family and to give them strength. When he finished praying, there had been silence for a moment. No one had heard Josh pray spontaneously before. Josh had been a little embarrassed, but it had felt good.

"That was a very nice prayer, Josh," said his mother after a moment. Josh felt his cheeks turn red. Kendra was looking at him, but she didn't say anything.

"Thanks," was all Adam said.

After dinner, Josh and Adam walked up to Josh's room. Josh stood examining his collection of compact discs, wondering which one to play for Adam.

"Don't you have any heavy metal?" Adam asked.

"No, I don't," Josh answered, wishing he had so that he could answer his friend's request. Josh grabbed a compact disc that he hadn't listened to much. His grandparents had given it to him for Christmas. "I like this song 'Angels Watching over Me' and some of the other songs on this disc," Josh said, putting the Amy Grant disc into his CD player. "Have you ever heard it?"

"I don't know," Adam answered, as the music started. Adam didn't really seem to be listening to the music, his mind was preoccupied with thoughts about his parents and their separation. "I suppose I'll live with my mom. Brent spends most of the time with his mom, and then his dad has him every other weekend." The mood became cold in Josh's room. Adam continued, "Brent says it isn't so bad because now his mother gives him almost anything he wants." Adam chuckled and then continued, "He says he thinks she feels guilty, so she tries to make it up to him by giving him things. I wouldn't mind that."

Josh knew that wasn't the way Adam really felt, but he didn't say anything. During the silence, one song finished and another started. Words about turning your back on the devil and living for Jesus came from the speaker. For Josh it was as though he had heard the words for the first time.

Adam continued, "Yeah, Brent—his mom just bought him this awesome skateboard, and he says his dad is getting him a dirt bike."

Josh heard other lyrics from the song— words about living your life for Jesus.

"What kind of music is this?" Adam asked.

Josh was suddenly embarrassed. "Well, it's Amy Grant. She's a Christian."

"I don't get into church music," Adam said, overemphasizing the word church.

"It's not church music," Josh said, defending his selection of tunes.

"Well, do you have normal music? "

"I don't really get into that kind of music," Josh said, reluctant to admit it, but suddenly feeling better that he had.

"That's cool," Adam said, "to each his own."

Josh started to feel like he had the day he and Adam had argued about drinking and watching pornographic movies. They were still friends, but Josh felt like they were heading in two different directions.

How does being a committed Christian affect your relationship with other people? How does it affect your relationship to your world? We've looked at how being a Christian changes what you think about the real you, and how it changes how you act in the family, now let's see how being a Christian affects the way you act outside your family—with the family of humankind.

Many of the same principles that we covered in the last chapter apply here as well. Our same A B C model is used:

 Situations and circumstances occur.

Because we know how to P L A Y (pray, learn, act, yield), we allow God's Spirit to guide us, and we react to the situations and circumstances according to His will.

 God has promised that when we are faithful to His will, He will bless the results.

God's Word tells us that we will reap what we sow. In other words, if we want to experience love and joy and peace, we have to plant the seeds of love and joy and peace. Real love and real joy and real peace are only available through God's Spirit. This is the fruit we are given when we surrender the B area of our lives.

God's Word also tells us that even if the situations that occur—the A's—are really bad, if we yield to His Spirit (B), He brings something good (C) out of the bad A's. Romans 8:28 again: "We know that in all things God works for good with those who love Him, those whom He has called according to His purpose."

What does that mean? Does that mean that Josh's grade in algebra suddenly goes from an F to an A? Does that mean the zits on Josh's face disappear? Does that mean Adam's family experiences immediate healing, and everything turns out happily ever after?

The answer to all these questions—except the last one—is no. Being a Christian doesn't exempt us from bad A's—but as far as "happily ever after" is concerned, we do have some pretty awesome assurances about that:

> All this is for your sake; and as God's grace reaches more and more people, they will offer to the glory of God more prayers of thanksgiving.
> For this reason we never become discouraged. Even though our physical being is gradually decaying, yet our spiritual being is renewed day after day. And this small and temporary trouble we suffer will bring us a tremendous and eternal glory, much greater than the trouble. For we fix our attention, not on things that are seen, but on things that are unseen. What can be seen lasts only for a time, but what cannot be seen lasts forever. (2 Corinthians 4:15–18)

Maybe it is hard for you to imagine that your troubles are temporary. Or maybe you haven't experienced all that much trouble. But what Paul is saying here is that life is really very short, and the thing that matters is not how much we have invested in this world, but, rather, how much we have invested in the next. So how do we make investments that last forever? That's where servanthood comes in—living out your Christian faith and commitment in the way that you treat other people—the way you live in the world. It's that life dedicated to God's love—knowing Him and making Him known.

We must never give up living the Christian life. Sometimes it is easy to get frustrated, and we begin to wonder if it's worth it. We watch some of our friends who have no time for God, and they seem to be having a lot more fun than we are. This is when we must remember that the Christian life requires patience. Many of the rewards God has promised us are yet to come. The Bible tells us it is like a farmer who plants his crops. The farmer must be patient for the harvest. As we follow Christ daily and seek to do His will, we are planting seeds in the soil of His love. The crops will grow. We will reap the harvest of eternal life, and we live with Christ forever.

Some of the rewards are more immediate, however. As we said, God has promised that those who are spiritual will bear the fruit of the Spirit: love, joy, peace, patience, kindness, goodness, faithfulness, humility, self-control (Galatians 5:22–23).

Living the Christian life isn't always easy. Satan will always try to derail us and get us to do things his way. There will always be that struggle in the B area of our lives. As you grow up you face many challenges that will test your faith. How are you going to handle the dating situation? What about lust? What about sex? What about drugs and alcohol? What about tobacco? What about dishonesty and lying? Is it okay to cheat on a test? How are you going to talk? What words are you going to use to try to impress others? What music and movies and television will you watch and listen to? What clothes will you wear? Who are you trying to impress, anyhow?

You see, the committed Christian isn't worried about impressing the world. The committed Christian wants to live for Jesus Christ. Remember what the people in charge did to Jesus? You, too, might feel persecuted for being His follower. So, is it worth it? Yes. Without one doubt. Yes!

I remember a boy in my youth group one time who asked, "You mean being a Christian is really going to change what I do with my life?"

"Most certainly," I answered.

"Gosh, man," he said, "I believe in God, but I don't want to get carried away with it."

I looked at him. "The Bible says that even the devil believes in God, so how are you any different than the devil?"

"Yeah, I know," he answered, (I wondered if he really did), "but, come on, you don't have to go overboard."

Dear reader, what do you think? Can you go overboard for God? What about Adam? Who is God to him? What role does God play in his life? What about Josh? What's happening to him? Can you see how Josh is beginning to realize that God is far more than "someone way up there who doesn't really care"?

God cares! He cares about the big questions you have to face in life. He also cares about life's everyday circumstances. He wants to be intimately involved in every decision you make. This is a faith that works.

When you have this type of faith it produces results. These results affect the way you see the world:

1. You will see every person as someone God loves.

That drunk in the gutter? God loves him as much as He has ever loved anyone.

Those homeless people who live on the streets? God loves them too.

What about the terrorists who kill innocent children? God loves them just as much as He loves the children.

God doesn't care about the color of a person's skin, how much money he has in the bank, whether she dresses in style. He doesn't care whether she is in the advanced classes or in the class for slow learners. He doesn't care whether he has long, greasy hair or is bald. God loves everyone equally—no matter what—no strings attached. That's unconditional love.

You've probably heard the term *agape* love—

that's the kind of love God has for everyone. It is love that is unconditional. We can't earn it. And it comes with no strings attached to it. It's the kind of love God wants to give us to share with each other. It's the type of love His Spirit fills us with when we continue to "PLAY" with Him and give Him the home-field advantage.

I can hear you wondering, I suppose this means that kid whose "guts I hate" is also a child of God's? You're right! And you're supposed to love that person too. Oh, you may not like what he does—but you must allow God's Spirit in you to love him anyhow. Jesus even loved the people that were putting Him to death. He said, "Forgive them, Father! They don't know what they're doing."

How do you perceive other people? Remember that your perception is determined by your values, your attitudes, and your needs. What value do you place on other people? What attitude do you have toward others? Do you realize how you need others to join you and work with you in accomplishing the task that Jesus has set out for you?

Jesus told a story about Judgment Day. For people who don't believe in Him, it's a pretty frightening story! He said:

> "When the Son of Man comes as King and all the angels with Him, He will sit on his

royal throne, and the people of all the nations will be gathered before Him. Then He will divide them into two groups, just as a shepherd separates the sheep from the goats. He will put the righteous people at His right and the others at His left. Then the King will say to the people on His right, 'Come, you that are blessed by My Father! Come and possess the kingdom which has been prepared for you ever since the creation of the world. I was hungry and you fed Me, thirsty and you gave Me a drink; I was a stranger and you received Me in your homes, naked and you clothed Me; I was sick and you took care of Me, in prison and you visited Me.' The righteous will then answer Him, 'When, Lord, did we ever see You hungry and feed You, or thirsty, and give You a drink? When did we ever see You a stranger and welcome You in our homes, or naked and clothe You? When did we ever see You sick or in prison, and visit You?' The King will reply, 'I tell you, whenever you did this for one of the least important of these brothers of mine, you did it for Me!'

"Then He will say to those on His left, 'Away from Me, you that are under God's curse! Away to the eternal fire which has been prepared for the Devil and his angels! I was hungry but you would not feed Me, thirsty but you would not give Me a drink; I was a stranger but you would not welcome Me in your homes, naked but you would not clothe Me; I was sick and in prison but you would not take care of Me.' Then they will answer Him, 'When, Lord, did we ever see You hungry or thirsty or a stranger or naked or sick or in prison, and we would not help You?' The King will reply, 'I tell you, whenever you refused to help one of these least important ones, you refused to help Me.' These, then, will be sent off to eternal punishment, but the righteous will go to eternal life." (Matthew 25:31–46)

Simply put: we love Jesus only as much as the person we love the least. Think of a person you don't love very much. Hey, that person could be Jesus!

Does that sound tough? It is. But we can remember the story of the Good Samaritan again. Like the man on the road to Jericho, we have a Good Samaritan too. Jesus is our Good Samaritan who always sees us as His neighbor. He forgives us when we fail, and His great love for us will help us see the needs of the "unlovely" people around us.

As Josh grows in his walk with Christ, how will his faith continue to influence how he thinks about himself and how he acts in his family? How will it influence how he acts at school? Josh doesn't like Paul much. Remember Paul, the kid who is such a stud at everything? How will growing in Jesus change Josh's view of Paul?

Last night I caught a burger at McDonald's. I was sitting eating it when a group of kids walked in. They stood right in front of the booth where I was sitting. They all had weird haircuts with dirty sayings shaved onto their heads. One head told me what to eat, and I didn't like it much. The same kid had these words sewn into his jacket in bright red letters: "I love everybody but you."

As they looked around McDonald's to see what was happening, they talked among themselves. Their language was filled with profanity. I didn't like it much, either. One lighted a cigarette and blew the smoke out of his nose. They all lit up, and it made me angry because I was sitting in the No Smoking section.

I thought about this chapter I was writing for this book. Is God's love really real? Did God really mean what Jesus said? Am I really expected to love these kids who are telling me to eat excrement? I stopped right there and said a prayer for those kids. I started to see them in a much different light. I saw that they were searching—trying hard to impress someone. I saw them as people who, for some reason, were angry at the world and wanted the world to know about it. I saw them as God saw them: precious human beings for whom He sent His Son Jesus to die. Jesus died for them.

Perhaps you think I was judging these kids? No, judging someone means deciding their worth and value. Only God can do that. There was no doubt in my mind that in God's eyes, these kids were of great value, and I felt the same love toward them that God did. But the Bible also says that you will know people from the type of fruit they produce. If you look at a tree and see that it doesn't have any apples on it, and you say "That tree doesn't have any apples," you're not judging the tree. If however, you say "That tree is no good and should be cut down," then you're judging the tree.

Suddenly, I had a burden for these kids. I wanted to tell them how much Jesus loved them. I wanted them to know how special they are to God. I wanted them to know that God has a plan and a purpose for their lives. I wanted to tell them that everything that they are looking for can be found in God. I wanted to tell them that I needed them to help me spread His love.

But I never got the chance. They looked around the restaurant for a few more moments as though they were looking for someone they didn't find, and then they exited. I listened to their foul mouths as they walked out the door.

I never had the chance to talk to these young people, but there will come times when God will open the door for you to share your faith. Most of the time we share it through our actions, but there are times when we must come right out and tell people with our lips about who Jesus is and His plan for our lives.

You will do this because you see others as God sees them. Consequently, . . .

2. You will love your neighbor as yourself.

Remember the story of the Good Samaritan that we read earlier? From that story we learned that Jesus said, "Love your neighbor as much as you love yourself." Jesus is telling us in the story that our neighbor is anyone who is in need. We've already seen that it is easy to find certain people who are difficult to love, but our commandment in Christ is to love everybody as much as we love ourselves.

Who are some of your "neighbors" who have needs? Realize that everyone has needs. Remember that we included in the list of basic needs the need to be loved. Everyone needs love. Do you know anyone in your school whom others put down and make fun of? How could you befriend that person and show her or him God's love? (Your teachers need love too . . . does that surprise you, coming from a teacher? Now, principals—they don't need any love! Ha!)

Most schools are notorious for their cliques— their exclusive groups of students. These groups are formed because people in the groups share common interests and behavior. There are the "brains," the "nerds," the "party animals," the "jocks," the "brown-nosers," and lots of other cliques. They have different names in different schools, but they exist as surely as schools exist. Often times, real communication between people only occurs with others in their clique.

Adults have cliques too. They may not be as noticeable, but they certainly exist. Even churches can become cliquish.

How do you think Jesus feels about cliques? He said, "Love your neighbor as much as your love yourself." He didn't say: "Love only those who are in your clique, and have as little to do with those outside your clique as possible!"

How important is this commandment to love your neighbor as much as you love yourself? Look what the Bible says: "The commandments, 'Do not commit adultery; do not commit murder; do not steal; do not desire what belongs to someone else'—all these, and any others besides, are summed up in the one command, 'Love your neighbor as you love yourself.' If you love someone, you will never do him wrong; to love, then, is to obey the whole Law" (Romans 13:9–10).

It's the only law you need . . .

Another way of saying the same thing? Check this out . . .

3. Treat others in the way you would like to be treated. Some people call this "the Golden Rule." Jesus said, "Do for others what you want them to do for you. This is the meaning of the Law of Moses and of the teachings of the prophets" (Matthew 7:12).

It's pretty basic. Would you want others to gossip and spread stories about you? Do you like it when people try to throw stones in your path and discourage you? Do you like it when people steal from you or treat you unfairly? Of course not. So treat others in the way you'd like to be treated. Be an encourager. Remember to look for the things that are good and pure and holy.

Using our A B C's, we see the following as it relates to 1, 2, and 3:

 Situations occur. Circumstances happen. People are sometimes mean and cruel. Things are often unfair. We are hurt. We feel taken for granted. We don't like being walked on.

 We P L A Y. In the process of yielding to God's Spirit, we see things His way. We see the negative circumstances and situations as opportunities to grow closer to God.
James 1:2–4 says, "My brothers, consider yourselves fortunate when all kinds of trials come your way, for you know that when your faith succeeds in facing such trials, the result is the ability to endure. Make sure that your endurance carries you all the way without failing, so that you may be perfect and complete, lacking nothing."

As a result of yielding, we see others as our neighbors who have needs and whom God has called us to serve.

As a result of playing on God's home court, His Spirit helps us develop an attitude toward others that says, "However I would like to be treated is the way that I'm going to treat others." Rather than "I'm going to do it to others before they do it to me," or "I'm going to do it to others because they did it to me first," we yield to the Spirit's guidance.

 This is what occurs as a result of doing it God's way. Our lives won't become magically happy. But we know God is ready to help us and strengthen us. Our lives will be filled with the good fruit He has promised.

No, it isn't easy living like Christ. Much of the world tries to convince you to do otherwise. But you mustn't give up. Here are some suggestions to help you:

1. Remember to P L A Y. As you pray, God will give you assurance that you are on the right track and will give you encouragement to carry on. Remember to adore Him, confess to Him, thank Him, and bring your supplications (your requests) to Him. All these "ACTS" of prayer are essential. Confession is very important because we know that sometimes we will fail, and yet His Word tells us that "if we confess our sins to God, He will keep His promise and do what is right: He will forgive us our sins and purify us from all our wrongdoing" (1 John 1:9).

As you continue to learn through Bible study, the fellowship of the church, through Christian books and music and prayer, you will learn more about God's love. It's like learning to play the piano—the more time you spend practicing, the better you get. Not learning is like trying to put a model plane together without following the directions. As we learn more, God's will becomes more and more clear for our lives. As we see God's love in action, it is easier to love those around us.

Don't just talk the talk, but walk the walk. This is where acting on your faith begins. This is where all the head knowledge becomes heart knowledge, and you really begin to live like a believer. This is only possible if we . . .

Yield. This is where push comes to shove. Here is where the battle rages with the two powerful forces fighting for control of your life. Are you going to yield to God, or are you going to yield to Satan? You can't walk down the middle and only be lukewarm. That's the same thing as yielding to Satan.

Look what God says about being lukewarm as far as yielding is concerned: "I know what you have done; I know that you are neither cold nor hot. How I wish you were either one or the other!

147

But because you are lukewarm, neither hot nor cold, I am going to spit you out of my mouth!" (Revelation 3:15–16).

P L A Y God's way. In Christ, He provides you with everything you need.

2. Just as you set up a family altar, try to establish an altar at school. Who are the kids that share your commitment to Christ? Network with these kids. Find opportunities to get together before, during, or after school to have prayer and devotional studies. Recent court rulings allow Bible clubs in school and other expressions of religious practice. Take advantage of this freedom.

3. Turn your back on the deceiver! Live like a believer! Let's elaborate a bit on what we just discussed in the section on yielding and get a bit more specific to see what things can help us yield. One of them is mentioned in number 2 above: Fellowshiping with other believers. You have your altar at home. You can establish an altar at school. But . . .

Don't forget the altar at your church. Become a leader in your church. Support the activities of your church. What needs are there in the church that you could help meet? What gifts has God given you to put to use in the church? This may include, but not be limited to, singing in the choir; supporting the church with your money (yes, your money); being a leader in your youth group; praying for the leaders of your church—the pastor, the Sunday school teachers, the musicians, the janitors; visiting someone from your church who is in the hospital or a nursing home; helping clean the church. These are only a few of the ways to get involved in your church. What are some of the others?

Ask God to show you what areas of your life He's unhappy with, and then be willing to let God help change these areas. For instance, ask God, "God, what things do I do that displease You or make it difficult to live for You?" Be ready to hear God's answer. He may tell you that you need to work on controlling your tongue or your temper. He may tell you that He is unhappy with some unclean thoughts on which you've been dwelling. He may tell you to be nicer to your brother or sister. He may tell you to study harder—God wants you to do your best at everything you do.

God may show you that He wants you to be more vocal for Him. He wants you to tell others about Him. Some people may never know unless you tell them. Adam may never know Him unless Josh tells him.

As God shows you these areas of your life that need work, and as you yield to Him in these areas, you become more and more like Him. People will really begin to see God in you.

Yeah, really yielding to God may change the

type of music you listen to, the types of movies you go see, and what you do on Friday and Saturday nights.

Yielding to God may change the words that come out of your mouth. Yielding to God will change the way you obey your parents and others in positions of authority.

Yielding to God may change what you do with your boyfriend or your girlfriend.

Yielding to God may even change the way you dress.

Most certainly, yielding to God means that you see your role as a servant in the world.

Sound radical? It is! Christian faith is active and it is radical! It is the most radical thing in the world.

Well, what about Josh Anderson? And what about Adam? What about Mom and Dad and Kendra and Brent and Paul and Kari? What about me? What about you?

The question is the same for every one of us: So, what are you going to do with God? Remember that to not make up your mind is making up your mind. It's up to you to decide whether you are going to let God's Spirit lead you into an active faith that really matters. God will not force His way into your life. True love can't be forced. Only you can give Him the home-field advantage in your life.

Josh is starting to see that God really does exist. Josh is starting to put his faith in God to work. He doesn't have all the answers yet, but he sees the great love God has for him and is willing to trust God for what he doesn't know. The Bible tells us that even a mustard-seed sized faith can move mountains.

Who knows? Maybe someday Josh will even get up enough courage to share his faith with Adam.

God loves you, dear friend! So, what are you going to do about it?